THE TIME IS COMI
EVERYTHING THAT IS COVERED UP
WILL BE REVEALED, AND ALL THAT IS
SECRET WILL BE MADE KNOWN TO ALL.
LUKE 12:2

First published 2022

ISBN: 978-1-9996171-1-0

ACKNOWLEDGEMENTS

It took many amazing and brave people to make this book possible.

The tragic and horrific murder of fourteen-year-old Jodi Jones will live with me forever. From day one, my sole motivation and involvement in this case has been to find justice.

The wrongful imprisonment of fourteen-year-old schoolboy, Luke Mitchell, had a massive influence on me. The way Luke Mitchell has conducted himself over the years is quite remarkable given what we, as a society, did to him.

The treatment of Corrine Mitchell has been nothing short of disgusting, but her love for her son and her tenacity in her defence of Luke, when the whole world was against them, is inspirational.

Firstly, I have to thank Dr. Sandra Lean for the literally thousands of hours of consultations, fact checking, and painfully going over old ground. Without, the book would not have been possible.

Secondly, thank you to Kathryn Londry for the months of work, proof reading and restructuring, as I changed the format again and again. As I'm dyslexic the work could not have been easy, but without it the book would have been a difficult read for some.

Thirdly, the late Dr. Brian P. Gordon, a criminal psychologist and criminologist, who tolerated my obsession, with hundreds of hours of arguments and consultations. These were invaluable to me and to the book.

Fourthly, to the many people who were brave enough to trust me and speak up about their concerns in this horrific case. Professional people who gave their time and opinions for free, and the local people who spoke out, despite knowing that doing so could bring trouble to both them and their families.

Fifthly, to my family members, including my late father Freddie, my daughter Chloe, and brother and sister, Gary, and Lisa, who have supported me throughout the years after I first spoke out.

Lastly, and least, the hack reporters who assaulted my character with lies in order to discredit me when I first spoke out in 2005. These smears just made me more determined not to give up on this case, which has brought me here today

FOREWORD

I was expelled from school at age 13, sent to a List D school at age 14, and labelled a teenage delinquent. After school I worked as a joiner in the construction industry, was in and out of trouble and police stations, and eventually ended up in prison, which is where I read my first book.

In 2002, I walked into an old fire station in Abbey Hill in Edinburgh, which was then being used by Second Chance Learning, in the hope that I could make up for lost time and pursue the education I had missed out on. Thankfully, the course was full, and I instead met Dr Kate Smith, who would introduce me to Plato Republic, Newbattle Abbey School and Mark Kane, a man who would later become a "suspect" in the murder of Jodi Jones.

In 2006, I started to work on potential Miscarriages of Justice that had occurred in Scotland, which is when I was first introduced to HMA v Luke Mitchell. In 2007, I started a post graduate course in law - accelerated LL. B – and, with the guidance of the late Bill Stewart, I started to legally investigate Luke's conviction.

This gives me over forty years of experience in the criminal justice system, with the last fifteen years being in law, specializing in cold cases, criminal appeals, and potential miscarriages of justice, investigating cases to ascertain whether or not justice had been denied. Having spent the last nineteen years involved in Luke Mitchell v HMA gives me the knowledge and confidence to write this book.

Before I agree to investigate any case, the accused must sign a contract which states if they lie to me, the investigation is immediately dropped. Since obtaining access to the case files in 2006, I can honestly say that at no time have I discovered any lies pertaining to Luke Mitchell.

JUSTICE

It is with a heavy heart that I believe Jodi Jones may be denied justice for her brutal murder. In my opinion, the police contaminated and botched the investigation so badly that the killer, or killers, and their accomplices may walk free from this horrific murder.

That is unless people have the courage to speak up, like the mother burning clothes in the Newtongrange area soon after Jodi was murdered, the boys on the moped, or members of the Jones family and others who have information which could help bring the truth forward and some justice for the guilty in this case.

Having said that, however, I think in Luke Mitchell v HMA there can be no real justice. Even when Luke Mitchell is eventually acquitted, which he will be at some stage, it's justice delayed, and justice denied. His life has been taken from him and will never be the same again. His poor mother's life has been ruined and she may never live to see Luke freed from prison.

INVOLVEMENT

Luke Mitchell v HMA is different from any other case I've worked on for several reasons. To start, the murder of Jodi Jones happened in the area I originate from, I had just graduated from Newbattle Abbey College, which is very close to where the murder occurred and, at the time of the murder, my daughter was the same age as Jodi. This case wasn't chosen by me, but fate which brought it to me.

On the 1st of July 2003 I was visited at my flat in Balfour Street, Edinburgh by Mark Kane, who had been a fellow residential student at Newbattle Abbey College. Despite graduating earlier, Kane and others were permitted to stay on as residents at the college during the summer vacation.

Jodi's murder was all over the news and the police were asking the public to assist, and keep their eyes open for possible suspects or anyone who may be suspicious. They said the murderer would have been in a struggle, agitated and looking to leave the local area. This description was a perfect fit for what I witnessed when Kane showed up at my door.

Mark Kane left the Newbattle area for the first time in almost a year to visit me. He had never been to my flat in Leith before, and I had seen him only days earlier. After he entered the flat Miss Jamie Nolan, who was living there before going to university that September, asked Mark to remove the sunglasses he was wearing. When he did it was plain to see he had scratches on his face. Both myself and Miss Nolan asked him how he got the scratches. He couldn't answer and when pushed, finally said he fell into a bush. In my opinion, they were scratches from a fight or struggle and didn't appear to be from a bush.

Kane's behaviour that day was both uncharacteristic and strange. Jamie Nolan and I had witnessed Mark Kane for over a year at college. We had seen him on drugs and drink and at his worst, but his behaviour that day was different. He appeared shaken and nervous. When he was in the flat, we asked him where he had been. He told us he had been in the woods surrounding Newbattle Abbey, where he consumed methadone, speed, hash, and Valium, as well as drinking lager. When we reminded him a wee lassie had been murdered, he left the flat soon after.

After he left, Miss Nolan and myself were concerned about what we had just witnessed. Conversations with Kane's friends at Newbattle and men from his school days heightened those concerns. They witnessed Mark as obviously agitated, very evasive, hyperactive, and also saw the scratches on his face. People were rightly suspicious.

I met Kane the next day, on the 2nd of July 2003, and persuaded him to go to the police, if for no other reason than to eliminate himself as a suspect. I dropped him off at the police station. He went in and the police told him they were busy at the time, but they would get back to him. Police notes confirm: *"to be traced and interviewed."*

Soon after the murder Kane reverted back to heroin use and moved back to his mother's house in the Gracemount area of Edinburgh, before showing up at Stirling University in September 2004, where I was studying law. His behaviour at Stirling brought back memories. In one incident he was violently stabbing a door in residence for unknown reasons. A blind student, who was in residence, became scared and complained to university staff. They knew I had been at school with Kane at Newbattle Abbey College and reached out to me to intervene.

Another time, during fresher's week, Kane got into an argument with a female student on his way home while drunk. This resulted in scratches on his face through her defending herself. This reminded me of the time he visited my flat and I asked him how he got on with the police in the Luke Mitchell case. He told me they hadn't bothered with him. That troubled me.

On Boxing Day 2004, Kane was coming off methadone and asked me to help him with the withdrawal symptoms. We took a walk up toward the Sheriff Muir. On the walk he admitted to me that he didn't have a clue where he was the day Jodi was murdered. He did remember running on Newbattle Road, but the rest of the day was a blur.

He understood fully why people would be concerned about him and the murder. We spoke at length about Luke Mitchell and his trial. I pleaded for him to speak to someone, even the media. I reminded him a wee boy was on trial and Mark could, and should, have been investigated and such an investigation might have ruled out Luke Mitchell. He told me *"Fuck Luke Mitchell."* I informed him then that I wasn't prepared to sit back and say nothing and that I was going to start speaking out.

I spoke at length to my late father, Freddie, who lived in the area and was a regular in pubs. He acknowledged that by me speaking out he may get `hassled` by the community. He wasn't bothered in the slightest at this however, and told me if they, meaning police and authorities, weren't listening, to shout louder. I thought my daughter, Chloe, same age as Jodi, would get aggravation if I spoke out so I spoke to her about that possibility.

She also couldn't have been more supportive.

Soon after, I was interviewed by two CID officers from Dalkeith police station in an office at Stirling University, where I told them about Mark Kane. The police were shocked that he hadn't been interviewed earlier. Genuinely that was all that was ever required - an interview to eliminate him from the inquiry. At the end of the discussion, I asked the police officers what their take was on the Luke Mitchell case. They informed me that there was a lot of doubt about the case, except from the investigating team.

While Luke Mitchell was at trial, I spoke to Jane Farquharson, Junior Counsel for Luke, at the door of the court. I was prepared to give her a statement there and then. That is until I saw Beaumont and Co entering the court. Prior to Luke's trial I had contacted Beaumont and Co, as they had been retained to represent him, to advise them about Mark Kane, a man similar looking to Luke Mitchell, who was in Newbattle Road and surrounding area on the night of the murder. They never got back to me. I went thereafter and gave a sworn affidavit to Solicitor Advocate Robbie Burnet. I stand by every word of that Affidavit.

In 2006, I met Dr. Sandra Lean, a criminologist, and Corinne Mitchell, Luke's mom, and explained to them about Mark Kane and him being in the area on the night of the murder. Later that year I had 30 plus boxes of case files on HMA v Luke Mitchell stacked in my spare room/office.

Dr. Sandra Lean is a criminologist from the area of Mayfield in Dalkeith, not far from where Jodi was murdered. At the height of the hate and hype, Dr Lean spoke up on behalf of Luke Mitchell and the way the boy was being treated, a `lone voice in the wilderness`. The backlash toward her was so bad she was threatened and spat on in the street, however she never gave up. A person suffering a Miscarriage of Justice can only hope and pray that someone like Dr. Lean takes up their case.

While doing my postgraduate in Law, I was lucky enough to get advice and tap into the top legal minds in Scotland as I studied HMA v Luke Mitchell. Those legal minds could not believe that a boy could commit such a horrific murder and leave behind no DNA or forensics.

In 2010, after graduating and persuading the Law Society that my past was in the past and that I had changed my life, I was entered as a Fit and Proper Person to practice law in Scotland. I went on to a traineeship with a law firm in Glasgow. My first client was Luke Mitchell, and I have been involved in the case, from a legal perspective, ever since.

In the nineteen years I've been involved, I have worked with some of the greatest legal minds in Scotland: Maggie Scott QC, {now Lady Scott} Claire Mitchell QC, and the esteemed John Scott QC. All three have spoken out about the wrongful conviction, which speaks volumes in my opinion. In fact, every legal professional I've worked with over the years all have grave concerns about the verdict in the Luke Mitchell trial.

Working with top forensic scientists, pathologists, criminologists, including Dr. Sandra Lean, psychologists, investigative journalists, retired or former police officers, and expert witnesses, I can honestly say that in all my time working on the case, I never met anyone, who after being shown the facts with a knowledge of the scene, believed Luke Mitchell was guilty of murdering Jodi Jones. All of these professionals believe that Luke Mitchell's conviction is a terrible case of a miscarriage of justice.

There are those who say Luke Mitchell is guilty *"because I read it in the Daily Record"*, or *"my granny's cousin lives next door to a woman who sells Judith Jones fish, and I'm telling you he done it"*, or *"he is guilty just because he is"*...or my own Diabetes nurse who claimed, *"they can't just put you in jail for no reason- there must be something"*.

Then there are the few who financially and personally benefited from the Luke Mitchell stitch up, and who have to protect their positions at all costs, such as police officers from the investigation team and their friends in the media. The hack reporter, a close friend of DS Craig Dobbie and who was strategically placed with the Jones family by police, fed the public lies, smears and trash to destroy a boy and his family, without a threat of evidence against them.

These hack reporters were "guardians" of information fed to them by the police and have continued to feed the lies to the public since 2003. Imagine for a second people with an agenda, making up complete falsehoods, total fabrications, putting them in a popular tabloid and you can do nothing about it as the "source" was a policeman's friend.

Paul Clark and David Whitehouse, Rangers Administrators, were *"treated worse than "terrorists"* by Police Scotland, in a similar fashion to Luke Mitchell, after they were falsely accused of fraud. The big difference between Mr. Whitehouse and Mr. Clark and Luke Mitchell, was that Clark and Whitehouse had money and power to fight back and defend themselves. Luke Mitchell had only his mother and was living in a small, middle class estate.

In writing this, I am not hoping to convince or change anyone's mind. I simply would like to ask some people to search their conscience and speak out about what they know or may suspect about what happened on the 30th of June 2003.

Scott C Forbes B.A.(Hons) LL. B, LP.

INTRODUCTION

On the early evening of June 30th, 2003, a fourteen-year-old schoolgirl named Jodi Jones was brutally murdered, and later found in a woodland strip adjacent to Roan's Dyke Path. This path runs from Easthouses, the village where Jodi lived, to Newbattle Road, where her boyfriend, Luke Mitchell, resided.

Jodi's mutilated body was discovered by Luke Mitchell, Stephen Kelly, Janine Jones, and Alice Walker. Janine was Jodi's sister, Alice Walker was her grandmother, and Stephen was Janine's boyfriend at the time.

Luke, the fourteen-year-old boyfriend, was made the one and only suspect by Dalkeith police officers investigating the case. On a hunch, a policeman thought Luke looked too `cool` and suspicious as he sat on his own on a pavement, petting his dog, as Jodi's family gathered together soon after Jodi was found.

A media frenzy followed and Luke, the fourteen-year-old boyfriend, was never out the papers. They claimed he was a goth, evil, Satan incarnate, and even went so far as to suggest he was having sex with his own mother. The media were permitted to write whatever they wanted as Luke hadn't been charged and there were no legal proceedings against him.

Eventually Luke was charged with the murder of Jodi Jones and, at the High Court in Edinburgh, he was convicted on purely circumstantial evidence and sentenced to life imprisonment, with a recommendation that he serves a minimum of twenty years.

During his seventeen years of imprisonment, Luke has always claimed he did not murder Jodi. He has refused to admit his guilt and refused any prison courses which could help him move on within the system. In my opinion, the fact that most prisoners and prison officials believe that he didn't kill Jodi says a lot. How can a person, an alleged horrific murderer, keep up an act while in prison for all those years? I don't believe it can be done. The other prisoners would suss him out in no time. Luke continues to fight to clear his name and, hopefully, bring the guilty to justice.

Nineteen years after the horrific murder of Jodi Jones, the truly horrific and evil murder was again brought to the public's attention with the recent Channel 5 Documentary, Murder in a Small Town. The documentary is based solely on evidence discovered during the investigation into the murder of Jodi Jones and highlights other suspects in the case who were never truly explored by Lothian and Borders Police.

The producers of the documentary asked two former police officers, John Sallens, and Michael Neil, with a combined experience of over 50 years which included crime scene management, to examine the case and, in particular, the investigation into the murder of Jodi Jones.

Some in the public, including reporters and members of the Jones family, complained the program was one sided and lodged complaints. Not one of these complaints was upheld but it made good headlines at the time. The complainants, in my opinion, had everything to fear from the documentary as it highlighted incompetence and lies.

The murder of Jodi Jones and the conviction of her fourteen-year-old boyfriend, Luke Mitchell, has hung over Dalkeith,

Edinburgh, and Scotland like a black cloud since 2003 because of both the nature of the brutal murder and the questionable conviction, which raised more questions than it ever provided answers. The police "investigation" was so absolutely shocking you genuinely couldn't make it any worse if you had deliberately set out to sabotage it.

After nineteen years questions are still being asked about the case, questions which should have been answered back in 2003-2004 and, as a result, no one involved in the case can move on and aren't permitted to grieve properly as there is still so much lingering doubt.

In my opinion, Detective Superintendent Craig Dobbie and others, media included, were criminally negligent in this investigation.

I cannot even begin to imagine what some of Jodi's family must be feeling, both those who are grieving and those with secrets to hide. I make no apologies for saying such. I can only hope that the ones who lied or gave false evidence in this case are genuinely worried that the truth is being exposed.

Day after day, after trying to come to terms with the horrific murder of the teenager Jodi, the family had to live with the "gutter press," who at every opportunity published sensational stories, irrespective of validity, highlighting the case in their attacks on Luke Mitchell.

However, while I have the deepest of respect for Jodi Jones and some members of her family, I also have serious reservations about others who I believe know much more than they are letting on. Some know they purposely lied to police at the time to impede the police investigation and thereafter to help smear and eventually convict Luke Mitchell. John Ferris is a prime example.

Ferris was a grown man, a known drug dealer, knife carrier, and bare faced liar with regard to the murder of Jodi Jones. The police permitted him to continue to sell drugs and destroy evidence in a murder investigation after he admitted to being at the scene at the time of the murder, in return for helping to paint a 14-year-old boy as some kind of villain. When Ferris eventually came forward on or around the 5th of July 2003, police weren't interested in the fact that he was at the locus at the time of the murder, or that he had helped destroy a moped that was seen to be there. They weren't interested in his drug dealing or the fact he carried a knife, or that he lied about his whereabouts at the time Jodi was murdered, ...they were interested in only one thing - Luke Mitchell.

I'm of the opinion that there are others in the Jones family and people connected to them who either know, or have suspicions, about what happened all those years ago.

Andrina Bryson, the woman who claimed to have seen Luke on Roan's Dyke Path as she drove past, lied when she said she didn't know the Jones family, and her husband and mother-in-law were complicit in those lies.

Judith Jones, Jodi's mom, helped to cover for her son,

Joseph Jones.

Alice Walker, Jodi's late grandmother, should have been charged likewise for impeding the investigation by advising Dickie and Ferris not to go forward, knowing that police were wanting to trace them. She was also guilty of misleading the police by withholding information about John Ferris and Joseph Jones. When Ferris informed the police that Alice Walker had told them not to go forward, Judith Jones turned against him, and he was subsequently threatened by Joseph Jones and forced to move out of Dalkeith.

Joseph Jones should have been charged with threatening Crown witnesses when he threatened John Ferris.

Gordon Dickie and his father David, lied to the police and others to cover up what they knew about what happened on the 30th of June 2003. Gordon Dickie and John Ferris should have been charged with perverting the course of justice for being a serious impediment to the murder investigation by destroying the moped, Ferris cutting his hair to change his appearance, and on o both of them being involved in allegedly burning clothes after they were seen at the scene around the time of the murder.

More importantly, after reports of a "stocky man" seen following Jodi on Easthouses Road on June 30, 2003, Joseph Jones, who fit that description, does not say where he was for the first five days of the investigation.

Steven Kelly and Janine Jones both changed their initial statements about the search party dramatically over time to fit the narrative.

The injustices suffered by Jodi Jones and Luke Mitchell are my only concern in this case. I have sympathy for Mrs. Mitchell, Judith Jones, and others, but my focus is specifically on Jodi and Luke. I am of the opinion that Jodi Jones was treated with utter contempt and total disrespect by Lothian and Borders Police, who failed miserably in investigating her murder.

Instead, with the help of the press, they smeared and destroyed a young boy and his family in order to *"get their man"*, while – in the words of their own liaison officer - they botched a murder inquiry.

As a society, Scotland should look at how it treats children accused of a crime. Without a thread of evidence, we as a society, permitted a child, a boy of 14, with no criminal record whatsoever, to be smeared with lies and trashed by police and their friends in the media for fourteen months before he was charged. You cannot treat a convicted paedophile in this country the way Luke was treated, as the paedophile has "rights." Where were Luke's rights?

Luke Mitchell was stitched up, framed, call it what you will, but the fact is Lothian and Borders Police, led by DS Craig Dobbie and assisted by his friends in the media, made a murderer out of a schoolboy because they had botched the investigation from the onset and knew the public wouldn't have accepted their failings.

The press, orchestrated by the police, resorted to unrelenting vilification of Luke Mitchell and his family. He was accused, without a thread of evidence, of incest and being a major drug dealer who had an obsession with the occult. All of this at a time when emotions were running high in his local community.

In my opinion, the Luke Mitchell case is a miscarriage of justice; the worst in Scottish Legal History, because both victims in this case were children.

Despite the murder of Jodi being one with a violent struggle, horrific injuries, and a large crime scene, the police got NO answers from their forensic examination. No DNA, no blood splatters, no fingerprints, no hairs, nothing. This is extraordinary, to say the least, from a crime scene such as this one. There was evidence which should have been tested but was not.

Both basic and critical to all crime scenes is the preservation of evidence and a police procedure which should be strictly observed. Yet the murder scene was destroyed, contaminated, and later sabotaged by being washed with bleach, all while it was being "protected" by Lothian and Borders Police.

Jodi Jones was left out all night, uncovered and open to the elements because the first pathologist on the scene was not fit enough to climb through the V break in the wall and too idle to walk a few hundred yards to access the locus from several other directions. This paints a picture of laziness and negligence, which sums up the police work in its entirety.

The police permitted evidence to be destroyed when they permitted witnesses who had cradled Jodi to go home without forensically examining them. They permitted others at the locus, including a police officer who had been at the body of Jodi, to leave without examining them or taking their clothes. Luke Mitchell was the only one forensically examined. Only Luke Mitchell had his phone taken on the night of the murder to be analyzed.

They trampled all over the crime scene, cutting branches in order to get better photos. They rolled Jodi onto a plastic sheet and dragged her more than 10 meters across the crime site. The mismanagement of the crime scene was shambolic to say the least.

From the 3rd of July 2003, four days after Jodi Jones was murdered and before police had a chance to trace the "moped boys" who were spotted at the locus at the time of the murder or trace the "stocky man" who was seen following Jodi on Easthouses Road or speak to Mark Kane, or carry out any real meaningful investigation, they made Luke the one and only suspect....

without a single thread of evidence.

The press and police targeted a schoolboy while totally ignoring or turning a blind eye to many others who should have been, at the very least, people of interest. Police had spoiled the crime scene, missed witnesses, permitted mopeds to be scrapped, clothes to be burnt, and had no other option but to stick with their only suspect, Luke Mitchell.

DS Dobbie, with the help of some in the media, used his position to frame a young boy consciously or unconsciously, for the murder of Jodi Jones and may, as a result, have prevented the murderer of Jodi from ever being brought to justice.

When Sky News interviewed Luke Mitchell and his mother, reporter James Mathews appeared to have been briefed by police on which questions to ask. This was an interview conducted at a time in the murder investigation when detectives had precious little or NO evidence whatsoever.

On the face of things, the police operation looked detailed and intense, such as travelling to St Andrews to speak to former pupils of Newbattle Abbey College, while failing to interview Mark Kane and others living at the college a few hundred meters away from the police station.

Two of the most senior police on the case travelled to the United States of America to seek assistance from the Federal Bureau of Investigation, only to ignore their conclusions and redact the report to stop anyone else viewing it. Speaking to the FBI, I learned the report was not available as it was the property of Lothian and Borders police and under confidentiality laws, so the findings could not be shared. However, the FBI were clear it was not Luke Mitchell who killed Jodi Jones and were very critical of Lothian and Borders Police. To obtain a new report a £30,000 retainer and £1000 an hour thereafter was required.

Despite the horrific nature of the crime, there is not one thread of evidence against Luke Mitchell. None. How can that be? It's impossible.

Jodi Jones was murdered, according to the police, at 5.15 p.m. on the 30th of June 2003. Also, according to their theory, Luke Mitchell was alleged to have attacked her in a frenzied assault, tied her up, stripped her, brutally mutilated her with over 300 wounds. He then had to leave the scene without leaving a trace, get home, three quarters of a mile away, in a busy middle-class suburb without anyone seeing him, change his clothes and scrub away any DNA before going out to play with his pals at 6 p.m. Less than an hour .... impossible.

While the police concentrated solely on Luke Mitchell, they were unknowingly assisting people known to Jodi. People who had lied to police and had destroyed evidence, were at the crime scene at the time of the brutal murder, but when questioned couldn't remember what they were doing at 5:15 p.m. when Jodi was being killed.

Some of these people were poachers, killers and torturers of animals and admitted large scale drug dealers, however all of this was ignored in exchange for statements against Luke Mitchell's character.

While Lothian and Borders police concentrated on the Goth culture and Marilyn Manson, they failed to investigate the culture of hunting, poaching and animal barbarity within Jodi's local community. Men who had a history in hunting, killing and mutilating animals, and experts in avoiding detection from police and gamekeepers, were never considered `suspects` despite their backgrounds, knowledge of the area, who were at the crime scene at the time of the murder and soon after, and their subsequent lies to police.

The woodland strip where Jodi was found, is approximately 900 m x 20 m. For such a small space there is a great amount of activity, including `gang huts` where people meet to drink, smoke, and hold occult meetings. The culture of the hunting and animal brutality is frightening. This includes badger baiting, killing foxes, rabbits, killing and burying greyhounds who can't race any more, and letting pit bull terriers kill greyhounds. All of this was happening regularly on this woodland strip......and all was ignored by police in this investigation.

Luke Mitchell was forensically examined on the night Jodi Jones was murdered. The forensic report said his hands, wrists, and ankles were dirty, his hair was unwashed, and had dirt residue under his nails. There was no attempt from Luke Mitchell to `scrub up`. The police would have been aware of this as they took his clothes and samples.

The police had ruined the investigation by permitting important witnesses to get away without being questioned and failed to forensically examine witnesses or phones. The police were so confident that their `hunch` was correct, they did nothing to investigate the murder of Jodi, relying on the belief that forensics would prove Luke murdered Jodi.

Can you imagine for a second how the police must have felt when the forensic report established that there was no DNA that could link Luke Mitchell to the crime of murdering Jodi Jones? A report which cleared him as a suspect – or should have cleared him.

The whole case had been focused on Luke Mitchell and they were waiting on a positive DNA report and instead got nothing. If DNA can and does prove guilt, then equally it can help establish innocence......not in this case.

MEDIA

It must be said from the start that despite Lothian and Borders Police and Craig Dobbie using the media to inform the public on anything they thought fit their narrative, they declined the offer of BBC Crime Watch to help catch the killer of Jodi Jones and to help possibly identify the "stocky man" who was witnessed in the area around the time of the murder.

DS Craig Dobbie, and one his mentors, former Deputy Chief Constable Tom Wood, were both involved in Scotland's most controversial and notorious murder investigations, and both used the media to full effect in helping to *"get their man"*, while at the same time promoting themselves and spinning police failures into *"great police work"*. And coincidentally, both are close friends to a hack reporter at the Daily Record.

Tom Wood led the investigation into the Worlds End Murders, and when speaking after Angus Sinclair was finally convicted, he was reported as working *"tirelessly over 40 years to see the killers of 17-year-old friends Christine Eadie and Helen Scott brought to justice"*.

What Wood, who was in overall command of the Worlds End murders, failed to mention was that Angus Sinclair was also Scotland's luckiest serial killer. Angus Sinclair, as a result of police failures and stitching up the wrong people, was permitted to go on and murder and rape children for years.

Sinclair was a predatory paedophile, rapist, and serial killer. Police had fitted up the wrong men for the murders and, in effect, gave Angus Robertson Sinclair a licence to kill.

Sinclair was linked to the murders of Anna Kennedy, 20, Hilda McAuley, 36, and Angus Cooney, 23, in 1977 but senior officers ignored the links. As a result, two men, George Beattie and Thomas Ross Young, were wrongly convicted of murders. If Sinclair had been investigated, lives would have been spared, and two miscarriages of justices would have been avoided.

George Beattie, 19, and reportedly a *"big safftie",* was convicted of murdering Margaret McLaughlin, 22, in Carluke. The leading detective, CS William Muncie shaped the evidence to get his man. Detectives now believe that Angus Sinclair was responsible for this murder.

The facts speak for themselves. There is no doubt that George Beattie could never have committed that murder.

In 1997, Frances Baker was raped and murdered in a similar fashion to seven other murders which occurred between 1977-78, including the Worlds End Murders of Helen Scott and Christine Eadie. The murders were committed the weekend in October prior to the trial of Thomas Ross Young. This case had striking resemblance to the Luke Mitchell media coverage in that every paper ran stories about the Worlds End murders and the trial at the same time, implying that Young was guilty of the crime. Young was a lorry driver, and a dangerous and violent serial sex offender who was, nevertheless, wrongly convicted of two murders with the help of the press. This gave Angus Sinclair a licence to go on and rape and murder women and children.

In response to two people being wrongly convicted, and women and children being raped and murdered, the police said, *"both murders were investigated by legacy force Strathclyde police resulting in convictions.".* Tom Wood went on to write a book about his great and tireless police work in catching Angus Sinclair. This mirrored DS Dobbie when he was boasting about his `great police work` in the Jodi Jones murder, despite it being a major failure from the outset.

DS Craig Dobbie learned his trade in the North Edinburgh drug scene, with a culture of "get your man at any cost". Dirty tricks and police informants were the norm. His boss, Tom Wood, was a close friend and business associate of the late Kenny Eriksson. Kenny was a convicted murderer who was involved in heroin dealing and organised crime. Wood was accused of helping Kenny Eriksson in his heroin trade, by tipping him off about any investigations into his criminal business in exchange for a portion of the profits. This attributed to Tom Wood not becoming Chief Constable.

When Wood attended Eriksson's funeral in 2015, he threatened legal action against the press if they printed anything *"scurrilous",* such as reporting a senior police officer attended the funeral of a murderer, which if printed would be, in his opinion *"absolutely disgraceful".*

If only the press had considered not spreading scandalous claims, lies and smears against Luke Mitchell to damage his reputation, stir up hate, and create a `lynch mob`, without which there would have never been a conviction of Luke Mitchell.

When Luke Mitchell was taken from his home on the on the 4$^{th\ of}$ July 2003 to be questioned "voluntarily" by the police, the world media was watching, tipped off by the police, and then hack reporters fed the public lies and hype. Headlines read such things as, *"no other suspects", "police aren't looking for anyone else".*

For approximately ten months before he was charged, the press painted a picture of an evil boy, by printing nonsense such as, *"he's shagging his ma", "Some have said that the relationship between Luke and Corinne Mitchell went beyond the `normal` mother-son bond", "The relationship was said to be extraordinarily physically close".* How can it be permitted, or even defended, when trash such as this is printed without a shred of evidence?

I originate from Danderhall, my sister lived in Easthouses at the time of the murder, my late Dad and family in Newton Village, and I have cousins in Mayfield, so I was very much aware of the `hate` which was being stirred up by the media in the local area. On the 5th of July 2003, the headline read, *"Evil has visited us and there is no peace now".* They were insinuating that "evil" was Luke Mitchell.

This was a witch hunt, by a lynch mob, controlled by the police and their hack reporting friends.

The predominant rumour in Dalkeith and Edinburgh at the time was that Luke Mitchell was taking the rap for his brother, Shane, who was a psychopath and a regular patient in the Rosslynlee Psychiatric Hospital. I now know this to be completely untrue.

The other rumour that made the rounds in the media was that the "evil" pair, Luke and Shane Mitchell, had hung a pet dog from a doorway in Newbattle Abbey Crescent, where they lived with their mother. This was utter nonsense, but the media had created such a frenzy of false information that the public believed anything at this point, no matter how ridiculous.

If Luke Mitchell had caused criminal damage or drove a car without a licence and legal proceedings had been raised against him, the media would have never gotten away with this smear campaign.

The media couldn't treat a convicted paedophile the way

they treated Luke Mitchell if the paedophile had ongoing or outstanding legal proceedings, but they could do what they did to a child who had never been in trouble with police or criminally convicted. The media were permitted to write whatever they wanted about Luke Mitchell because of the fact he wasn't a criminal.

On the 3[rd of] September 2003, there was massive media coverage of Jodi's funeral, and later of the visit to the gravesite by Luke Mitchell. The media, who had hundreds of photos of Luke Mitchell, chose to publish one where he looked the angriest as they ran with a story about how he had disrespected the grave by dropping a cigarette in the cemetery, and how Judith Jones had returned the flowers that he had left.

There was no doubt in the minds of the local community of Dalkeith that Mitchell was a *"beast"* who had murdered Jodi and who had turned up at the grave to show off the arrogance of an evil murderer. This opinion was based solely on what they were reading in the papers.

Heeding some bad advice, Luke Mitchell agreed to be interviewed on the day of the funeral and spoke to Sky News. When asked if her murdered Jodi, he responded, *"No, I never, I wouldn't think of it......In all the time we were going out, we never had an argument at all, never fell out or anything".*

The interview itself was set up like a police interrogation at a time when there was little or no evidence. James Matthews, from Sky News, sat much higher up than Luke and his mother Corinne, in a power position and one used to intimidate. Similar to a court of law where the judge sits above the accused. In my opinion, Matthews had been briefed by police to ask the questions that he did. In watching the interview, it appeared to be a form of entrapment. Whatever Luke Mitchell said was now on record and could and would be used against him.

Asking Luke about what life had been like for him the last few months, Luke responded, *"It's been worse than a nightmare"*. The worst part being when he *"found Jodi"*, and how he felt he was being tried *"by the media to see what the public decides"*, that the police said they had *"other suspects but I seem to be really the only person they are mentioning by name".* Matthews continued to ask pointed questions such as, could he account for his whereabouts between 5 p.m. until the moment Jodi was found? Luke was accurate in saying, *"you cannot keep a pin of every minute that you do something"* but the police *"expect people to".* Matthews continued by asking him about the burning of the clothes and the missing knife." *No"*, replied Luke, the burning of clothes *"wasn't us"*, instead a *"female relative of a suspect admitted burning clothes".* Allegedly, Mrs Helen Dickie was burning clothes at Reed Drive and Luke Mitchell, once again, had it correct.

He further said, *"not to believe everything you read in the papers".* If only people had listened to this.

This interview could easily be interpreted as a frightened young schoolboy, pressured into speaking out to anyone who would listen, at a time when the whole world was against him.
Then three days later on the 6th of September 2003, before Luke was charged with the murder, Newspaper headlines read, *"Jodi's boyfriend ` the only suspect".*

The fundamental principle for the right to a fair trial {article 6 ECHR} is the presumption of innocence. Luke Mitchell got neither. I draw attention to the case against Cliff Richard. The BBC filmed a police raid on his home after allegations of child abuse. It was later ruled that this filming had prejudiced proceedings and all police investigations were dropped. No such laws for Luke Mitchell.

It’s meant to be innocent until proven guilty.... well, unless you're a child in Scotland and the police and their friends want to create a murderer.

NO ONE TRASHES YOUR NAME, MORE THAN SOMEONE WHO IS AFRAID YOU WILL TELL THE TRUTH

In my opinion, based on nineteen years involvement in the case, the investigation carried out by Lothian and Borders Police officers was criminally negligent, aided and abetted by certain journalists, and one in particular who recently wrote, *"Cold cases attract amateur sleuths who think anyone with a Wi-Fi can solve crimes".*

According to this reporter, people *"have to stop investigating cold cases and leave solving crimes to the professionals."*

I believe both DS Craig Dobbie, and the reporter in his back pocket, knew that their actions were wrong and that they had created a child victim. The police had failed miserably in the investigation, destroying a crime scene, contaminating evidence, ignoring witnesses and suspects, and all they had to rely on were lies, smears and trash fed to the public through the media to create a monster of a schoolboy.

As soon as I had spoken to the police at Stirling University in 2005 regarding this case, attacks on my character started. Police who were tasked to investigate Mark Kane seemed more interested in destroying my character than investigating the murder of Jodi Jones. This didn't surprise me in the slightest. This tactic had been used throughout this case.

Anyone who dared speak out in favour of Luke Mitchell, or questioned the media involvement, were warned off by the police. On a visit to the locus in 2009 with the Miscarriages of Justice Organisation, and Neil Mackay, an investigative journalist and Editor of the Sunday Herald, Neil informed us that in his 25 years as a journalist, including investigating the troubles in Northern Ireland, he had never been warned off by the police and yet, when he had questioned the methods being used in the Luke Mitchell case, he was directly contacted by police and cautioned.

There were several corroborating witness statements regarding Mark Kane which confirmed he was in Newbattle woods on the day of the murder, had been acting strange on the days immediately following, and had large scratches on his face. Lothian and Borders Police appeared more interested in criticising my statement and my character, however, and used similar tactics which they had employed against Luke Mitchell.

Reading statements from staff at Newbattle Abbey College I couldn't believe just how pathetic the police were. One statement from an English teacher, Ms. McGillivray, who was asked if she had a copy of an essay about a man killing a \`woman in the woods\` written by Mark Kane, denied having one and this somehow confirmed Kane wrote no such essay. The tutor went on to say of me: *"he didn't like my class because he didn't like feminist poetry."* What feminist poetry had to do with the murder of a schoolgirl and my statements about Mark Kane having written that essay was puzzling, to say the least.

John Beckett, QC argued to the appeal court that a lecturer who receives thousands of essays in her career and who couldn't remember receiving one essay, *"confirmed Kane wrote no such essay"*. This wasn't even challenged by the defence.

THE MYSTERIOUS £50,000

The worst lie and character insult I faced was the story about the mysterious £50,000. This tale was invented by Lothian and Borders Police and fed to the Crown by reporters. The idea was preposterous. It was suggested that I told Mark Kane to `play along` and admit to the murder of Jodi Jones. He could then take the story to the media and we could receive £50,000.

John Beckett fed this story to the appeal court, with no challenge from the defence, despite it being manufactured by the police with not one shred of evidence to support their claim.

Mark Kane made several statements to police, posted on blogs and Facebook pages, claiming I was a thug and highlighting the fact I had been in prison when I was younger. He alleged I was somehow Dr Sandra Lean's "attack dog" and other less complimentary descriptions.

But at NO time did Mark Kane ever mention £50,000 or me proposing this idea to him. Not once. This was nothing more than a smoke screen by Lothian and Borders Police to discredit a member of the public who had concerns about a suspicious man in the area when Jodi was murdered. This was because not interviewing Mark Kane highlighted just how sloppy and lazy the investigation into the murder of a schoolgirl was. It was easier to try and demean someone questioning their methods than accept any wrongdoing.

Despite Mark Kane being in Dalkeith Police station on the 2nd of July 2003, and people bringing him to the attention of police, the police failed to interview him until early 2006. They had several statements about his behaviour, scratches on his face, and being in the area at the time of the murder, yet totally ruled him out and he was cleared of any involvement by police.

The same hack reporter who had been instrumental in spreading falsehoods about Luke Mitchell for her friend, Craig Dobbie, was now repeating it with me.

This was the police tactic throughout - building a lie, feed it to their parrot reporter, and turn the public against the intended target.

The whole of mainstream media in this case really need to question themselves with regard to the reporting of an accused child.

A LIE CAN TRAVEL HALFWAY AROUND THE WORLD WHILE THE TRUTH IS PUTTING ON ITS SHOES

From the outset of this case, if a statement from a witness did not suit or fit in with the police narrative, the police kept going back to the witnesses until they got the statement they needed. The best example of this are the witness statements from the search party: Janine Jones, Stephen Kelly, and Alice Walker.

Reading their first statements, in comparison to their latter ones, you could be forgiven for thinking that the statements were from different people. They had changed so drastically, and all in favour of the police theory.

When serious investigative journalists, such as Neil Mackay, started to ask questions about the media coverage, they were contacted by police and warned to back off because Luke Mitchell was the killer. When the FBI were asked to use `fresh eyes` on the case and their findings didn't suit or fit in with the police investigation, their findings were just redacted.

When criminologist, Dr Sandra Lean, started to ask questions about the case as early as 2004, she was spat on in the street, received threats of violence, had bullying men turn up at her home making threats on her life, and all was accepted and permitted by Dalkeith Police.

In 2021, Channel 5 aired Murder in a Small Town, a two-part

series on the murder Jodi Jones. Professor Alan Jamieson and his staff from the Forensic Institute in Glasgow, along with two former police detectives, John Sallens and Michael Neill, with over fifty years of detective experience including crime scene management, were asked to investigate the murder of Jodi Jones and to examine if the original investigation could have been done differently.

The investigation, like any investigation, academic or criminal, should concentrate on the evidence, first and foremost.

The investigating team established that there was significantly more evidence pointing towards others rather than Luke Mitchell. They determined there was NO evidence whatsoever against Luke Mitchell.

John Sallens concluded it was not Luke Mitchell who murdered Jodi Jones. He expressed that Luke had *"suffered a serious miscarriage of justice"* and been let down terribly by the Scottish Legal System. These are sentiments with which I completely concur, although I will go one step further and suggest that Luke Mitchell was framed, and made a murderer of, by Lothian and Borders Police.

In the series Luke Mitchell told investigators, *"I was the local weirdo, it was easy to put it on me,"* and how DS Craig Dobbie and others had said during the interrogation to, *"confess you little bastard".*

Despite years of media slurs and untruths, and the pressure that goes along with that, and spending seventeen years in prison after being wrongly convicted of such a heinous crime, Luke Mitchell continues to maintain his innocence. Very few human beings could take such pressure if they were guilty, in my opinion, and the majority of the prison population and institution staff appear to agree. You cannot `con` prisoners for seventeen years.

Luke Mitchell was straightforward in his statement, *"I cannot be more clear, I absolutely did not kill Jodi Jones and I have been locked up for a crime I did not commit. I will not admit to something I have not done. I want to clear my name."*

I don't know anyone who wasn't emotionally affected, or at least moved to question the conviction after watching the series, except those who feared the truth and those with things to hide.

I did hear several times that the series was one sided and that they didn't investigate Luke Mitchell. I argued it wasn't biased in favour of Luke Mitchell because the research team weren't working for Luke Mitchell, or attempting to clear his name. They were instructed to simply delve into the case from scratch and, after examining the evidence, declare their findings. There was, and is, NO evidence against Luke Mitchell, and what evidence there was pointed towards others.

The case was now at a stage where forensic scientists, forensic pathologists, polygraph experts, crime scene managers, senior detectives, lawyers, QCs, Advocates, and the FBI were all saying Luke Mitchell was wrongly convicted of the heinous crime of murder.

Over the years I've thought about the beast of a person, or persons who murdered Jodi Jones. They must have been incredibly mentally unwell and could not be of normal mind. However, I must say those who made fundamental mistakes in the investigation, perpetuated lies and defamed a child in order to build their career are every bit as bad, if not worse, than the `sick` killer or killers of Jodi Jones, in my opinion.

While the vast majority of people were, at the very least, questioning the conviction of Luke Mitchell, even the ones who believed he was guilty, the ones who were afraid of the truth came out in defence and promotion of themselves, establishing what many had known all along - that the police and certain members of the media thought themselves above criticism or questioning.

The initial reaction from some in the media was not to question the facts of what had been claimed, but to attempt to discredit the two investigating former detectives asked to investigate the murder of Jodi Jones. Shoot the messenger rather than listening because the message highlighted the failings of police and agents of the media.

When they were unable to ruin the character of the investigators, they turned their attention to me. They sent a hack reporter to Mark Kane's dying mother and implied that the people who reported Mark Kane for being in the area at the time of the murder and on drugs, were fraudsters, and that the "old one of £50,000" resurfaced. Luke Mitchell faced these lies and rubbish media from day one of this case. How he and his mother coped with the pressure is beyond me.

Based on their reaction to the television series, it was evident to me that members of the Lothian and Borders Police and certain members of the media had not a care for the victims, only for money and their careers.

Jane Hamilton, a hack reporter, had from day one been spreading lies, smears, and conjecture in the case to support her close friend, DS Craig Dobbie. When esteemed professionals with far greater experience, education, and knowledge say something is wrong, it is only a truly arrogant and ignorant individual who totally disregards their opinion. Which is exactly what Ms. Hamilton did, while making herself the `victim` and the social `hero` at the same time, in response to the TV Series. She told readers that she had been made into public enemy No 1, the *"pantomime villain"*, who was the *"lone voice in the wilderness while all around me the baying mob were calling for my head"* and how she was *"standing up against the court of public opinion"*.

There are many victims in the Jodi Jones murder case with Jodi Jones being the primary and most important one. Some members of Jodi's family are victims. So are Luke Mitchell and his mother. Jane Hamilton certainly isn't one of them.

Complaining about all *"manners of slurs, vitriol and downright rudeness slung her way,"* you could be forgiven for thinking she was describing exactly what she had done to Luke Mitchell and his mother from 2003-2021.

The hypocrisy, lack of self-awareness and the one-sided and biased reporting have been evident since 2003. It was pointed out to readers of a certain publication that Luke Mitchell had been convicted by a jury and had failed on four appeal attempts, painting a picture of justice being served while failing to highlight that miscarriages of justice occur regularly.

Some weeks later that same publication reported on the Miscarriages of Justice of Joe Steele and Tommy Campbell *{Ice Cream Wars}* who were fitted up by police, spent sixteen years in prison, failed in several criminal appeal attempts, and it was now being covered without an ounce of irony.

Nevertheless, Ms Hamilton absolves herself of any wrongdoing, asking the question; *"what heinous crime have you committed this time, Hamilton?."* The heinous crime of stitching up a child and putting him in jail for a murder he didn't commit comes to mind.

The publication's printed reaction to Murder in a Small Town stated, *"Many - including senior police officers and Jodi's family - are angry that the TV documentary failed to point out key facts."*

Let's examine the `facts` that were not mentioned in the two-part series, and hopefully highlight the media bias that has been evident in this case since the beginning.

"The hard facts that prove Luke Mitchell murdered Jodi Jones in Cold Blood" from an article published in The Daily Record.

"Here (this publication) answers the then-key questions often raised by those who think Luke Mitchell should be cleared."

"Why wasn't Luke's DNA on Jodi?"

"Luke's DNA was actually found on her bra and her DNA was found on Luke's trousers, but in an agreement between the Crown and defence team, led by Donald Findlay QC, it was decided the issue of DNA wasn't relevant as the pair were in an intimate relationship. The Crown weren't going to say DNA made him the killer as it was expected his DNA would be on Jodi. DNA in this case wouldn't prove innocence or guilt".

Anyone reading this with any knowledge of criminal justice, forensics, or DNA evidence, would laugh at the above statement had the case not been so serious. This is media spin.

Jodi Jones' DNA was found on a pair of trousers belonging to Luke Mitchell. The trousers were in a holdall at his father's house in Livingston, a home he hadn't been to for at least a fortnight prior to the murder of Jodi. The evidence was, therefore, deemed irrelevant and agreed to be dismissed.

The DNA found on her bra was a mixed profile of three people, Jodi Jones being one. You could not *"rule out"* Luke Mitchell, but you could not rule out the DNA of Joseph Jones, John Ferris, Gordon Dickie, Stephen Kelly, or DS Craig Dobbie for that matter. Nevertheless, the trial Judge, Lord Nimmo Smith QC, permitted the Jury to hear *"you could not rule out Luke Mitchell."* Another spin from hack reporters.

The only direct DNA link to Jodi Jones was sperm, belonging to Stephen Kelly, found on Jodi's T-shirt. Stephen was Jodi's sister's boyfriend and a member of the search party. Kelly was permitted by police to go home without his clothes being taken for forensic examination after Jodi's body was found. These clothes were later washed by Alice Walker.

Any other murder case, with a person's sperm being found on the deceased clothes, would make that person a `suspect` or at least a person of interest. Not in this case. Stephen Kelly could not explain how his sperm was on Jodi's T-shirt, so the police gave him the explanation that was required. Jodi must have borrowed her sister's T-Shirt, and the `investigation` into Stephen Kelly was concluded. The problem with that theory is that Janine and Jodi lived in different houses and she would not have had access to the t-shirt.

Similar to the police taking David Dickie back to the murder scene with his dogs, on or around the 7th of July, after he had been there on the night of the murder. By taking Dickie back to the locus, the police had contaminated the DNA evidence (a blood like substance) found on his boots, and there closed the 'investigation ` against David Dickie.

DNA and forensic science have improved dramatically from 10 spikes in 2003, to 16 spikes in 2022, and the science is much more accurate. There are samples in the case, that if re-examined, could definitively prove who the murderer is.

Sadly, it's not an easy task to get access to those samples in order to carry out tests. The Crown considered the case closed, as they do in all miscarriage of justice cases, and refused access to evidence. It can take years of fighting in the courts to gain access.

"What about the witness who said she saw Luke and Jodi at the entrance to the path as she drove past then couldn't pick him out in court?"

"Andrina Bryson's evidence was considered an important element in the Crown's case as she came forward independently to say she saw a male and a female at the Easthouses part of Roan's Dyke at about 1650.

She described the male as wearing a khaki green, hip-length, fishing-style jacket. Its collar was up, and it had a pocket which was bulging. She picked out a photograph of Mitchell although could not identify him at court.

She was unable to identify the female whom she only saw from the back, but gave a description of someone with black, shoulder length hair, which seemed to be contained like a ponytail, wearing a navy-blue jumper with a hood and a pair of lighter trousers, which she took to be a pair of jeans. Apart from the jeans, the description fitted Jodi. The appeal court judges said that while her identification evidence was open to challenge there were elements that provided the basis for a valid identification of Mitchell as the male she had seen and Jodi as the female.

They said her evidence did not stand alone - it fitted that Jodi had left to meet Mitchell and they were in their regular 'rendezvous' point when spotted. The timings, they said, also fit. The prosecution claimed that had Jodi left the house and proceeded directly to the path, that she would have been there at the time of this sighting and asked the jury to accept that this was a sighting of Jodi and Mitchell.

Two other witnesses also identified Mitchell as the young man they had seen at the Newbattle end of the path around 50 minutes later."

Andrina Bryson was not an independent witness. She and her family were friends with the Jones and Walker families. She claimed she did not know the Jones family.

Jodi Jones was identified by the media at approximately 3 p.m. on the 1st of July 2003, and within a couple of hours Ms. Bryson had contacted the police.

According to John Ferris, Ms. Bryson's brother in-law, Mark "Bill" Bryson, was in Alice Walker's home on the morning of the 1st of July and, in discussing the murder, told them how his brother, not Ms Bryson, had seen a youth with *"long messy hair, wearing army clothes and big boots"* at the Easthouses end of Roan's Dyke Path. This conversation turned to Luke Mitchell, as he had previously been in the army cadets and the person claimed to have been seen was alleged to be wearing army style clothes. Bill then left Alice Walker's home to visit his brother and Andrina Bryson.

A couple of days after Jodi was killed, Mark "Bill" Bryson was in the home of Judith Jones and Alan Ovens speaking about the murder and Luke Mitchell.

Without Andrina Bryson, the police case wouldn't get off the ground. There were discrepancies about the time Ms Bryson travelled along Easthouses Road, based on supermarket receipts and cash line receipts. It was estimated she was on the Easthouses Road at around 4:55 p.m.

Anyone with local knowledge, or persons who had taken the time to drive along the route that Ms Bryson claimed to have driven, would know her claims were absurd. Under cross examination, Ms. Bryson claimed the Newbattle High School sign was on her left-hand side as she drove past the entrance to Roan's Dyke Path which meant she was driving towards Easthouses from the Newtongrange direction. To look down Roan's Dyke Path, the driver would need to turn their neck 180 degrees and it would be virtually impossible for a driver to see what Ms Bryson claimed to have seen and give details of clothes, hair and "a pocket bulging". That's absolute nonsense.

If she was mistaken about the direction she was driving and instead was driving from the Woodburn/Mayfield area instead, as her evidence suggests, she would get a better view of the path, however it would be nothing more than a passing glance as she drove by at 30-40MPH at best.

Ms. Bryson, in identifying Luke Mitchell, did so from a Polaroid photograph with a white background, inserted into a spread of other photographs with dark backgrounds, from a police folder. All the males in the folder were pre-teens and looked nothing like what was described by Ms. Bryson. Basically, the police targeted who she could pick from the photograph line up. Nevertheless, the jury, despite her not being able to identify Jodi or Luke Mitchell in court, accepted her testimony.

More importantly, they were not made aware of Mark Kane, who was in his early twenties and matched the age and description

Ms Bryson gave under oath. They were also not made aware of the "stocky man" seen following Jodi Jones along Easthouses Road, heading in the direction of the entrance to Roan's Dyke Path.

In 2010, solicitor, Graham Mann and myself tracked Ms Bryson to a house in Newtongrange. After making inquiries at her old property, she called our office. She was angry that we were trying to trace her but agreed to meet with us.

We assured her we only wished to ask a few questions regarding the identification of Luke Mitchell. When we arrived at her home, her husband and mother-in-law were in attendance. They were angry that we had been looking for them and Graham Mann reminded them that it was our job. Ms Bryson was as nervous a witness I had ever come across.

We asked why she couldn't pick Luke out in court considering the detailed description she had given of the man she had seen and subsequently able to identify from a photo. She wasn't sure, so I asked her if Luke had changed appearance, size, or weight from the alleged sighting to him appearing in court. Before Ms Bryson could answer me, her mother in-law interrupted by stating, *"that's it, that's it finished, no more questions."* We asked the reason why, but the meeting was quite obviously over. Ms Bryson has since moved to Australia, and it is my understanding she was again very nervous when she was tracked down in 2021 for the TV series.

"Two other witnesses also identified Mitchell as the young man they had seen at the Newbattle end of the path around 50 minutes later."

Rosemary Walsh and Lorraine Fleming believe they saw someone very similar to Luke Mitchell at approximately 5:45 p.m. at Newbattle Road, a fifteen minute walk from the alleged sighting of Luke Mitchell by Ms Bryson.

This gives a child, Luke Mitchell, 50 minutes to argue with his girlfriend, force her over a wall, murder her in a frenzied attack, strip her, mutilate her body, get home, change all his clothing, coat included, clean up without leaving so much as a trace of such a brutal murder, and be back on the Newbattle Road for Ms Walsh and Ms Fleming to see. Less than an hour.... I can conclude that Mitchell was not the killer of Jodi Jones.

Records show that Mark Kane told his close friends a lie, when he said he had been questioned by police as *"he had been seen running on Newbattle Road"* ......a man with a parka coat, with a similar hair style to Luke Mitchell seen on the road where Fleming and Walsh claimed to have seen Luke Mitchell ... and who had never been spoken to by police.

"And the missing jacket?"

"Luke was often seen wearing a distinctive parka style jacket and it was described by witnesses who saw him that night. When police searched his house, the jacket was gone.

The prosecution sought to link this with evidence that a log burner in the back garden of Mitchell's home had been used around 6:30 p.m. and 7:30 p.m. and later, at around 10:00 p.m. that night with an unusual smell as reported by neighbours".

Firstly, was it a *"khaki green, hip-length, fishing-style jacket"* as described by Andrina Bryson, worn by the man she claimed to have seen at Easthouses, or was it a ` *distinctive parka* ` described here by the reporter?

Witnesses Rosemary Walsh and Lorraine Fleming claimed to have seen a man who looked very similar to Luke Mitchell on Newbattle Road at approximately 5:45 p.m.

Ms Walsh describes the man's jacket, *"If I was to describe what type of jacket, I'd say a parka, but that's really just because of the length."* Lorraine Fleming described the jacket as dark in colour, possibly dark green, but the descriptions became more detailed the more the police visited. Both sightings were approximately 50 minutes after Ms Bryson claimed to have seen Luke Mitchell, and both descriptions were of a different man to the one described by Ms Bryson.

Lorraine Fleming described the man she witnessed at Newbattle Road, approximately two miles away, at 5:45 p.m. - looking like he was *"up to no good"*, who looked *"very much like Luke Mitchell"*, and had a *"Liam Gallagher hairstyle"*.

Her friend, Rosemary Walsh, who was travelling with her that day, described the man they saw on Newbattle Road as *"looking cheesed off."* Criminal psychologist, Dr Ian Stephen, described the murderer's profile as *"angry and disturbed."*
Different men, with different hair styles and different jackets were seen on that fateful day, if, in fact, Ms Bryson actually saw anyone.

A description commonly attributed to the "new suspect", Mark Kane, was that he had a hair style like Liam Gallagher from the television program Shameless, and who was, by his own admission, on Newbattle Road on the day of the murder. It had also been confirmed by several witnesses, including Dr Kate Smith, that he had a parka coat.

At approximately 5:55 p.m., Luke Mitchell was seen by people who knew him not far (300 meters) from where Ms Walsh and Ms Fleming had thought they had seen him on Newbattle Road. According to these particular sightings, he was wearing a dark green bomber jacket with an orange lining, baggy jeans, and light-coloured ski boots, all of which he was wearing later that night when he searched for Jodi. The police subsequently took all his clothing when he was taken in for questioning.

The log burner owned by the Mitchell family measured 10" x 14". To suggest that Corinne Mitchell, a woman with no criminal or forensic knowledge, somehow managed to burn and destroy a parka coat in this burner without leaving a trace of evidence is preposterous, to say the least. You couldn't burn socks in this fire pit let alone a parka coat. Moreover, there was no trace of fire accelerant.

Nevertheless, DS Craig Dobbie told the press, after Luke was convicted, *"...information which gave detectives cause for suspicion concerned the wood burning stove in the Mitchell's back garden"* He went on to say that witnesses had made reference to a *"long parka jacket."* allegedly owned by Mitchell. *"His mother said he had never owned one. When we searched the house, the parka was missing"*

Forensic examinations are integral and credible part of police investigations so if Mitchell had burnt, or attempted to burn a parka jacket, there would have been traces of it in the fire and garden. Of that I have no doubt whatsoever.

The best example I can give was the police investigation, a year after Luke Mitchell was convicted, into the murder of Vicki Hamilton by serial killer, Peter Tobin. Police examined a property sixteen years after the murder in the hopes of finding forensic evidence within the house. Four days before Tobin was convicted of murdering Polish student, Angelika Kluk, police submitted a purse belonging to Vicki Hamilton for DNA analysis and discovered DNA belonging to Peter Tobin's son who, as a three-year boy, sixteen years earlier, had bitten the purse which belonged to Vicki Hamilton, giving police a breakthrough. In the search of Tobin's former home, police found a knife in the attic and found tissue and DNA belonging to Vicki Hamilton.

Forensic science was found in the above mentioned case after sixteen years, yet we are expected to believe that a child, with no criminal or forensic knowledge, was able to frenziedly murder his girlfriend, mutilate her body, enter his house covered in blood and other forensics, clean up, burn clothes including a parka coat, in less than an hour, and not a trace of DNA or forensics were ever found. It's impossible.

There was, however, a report in the local paper, the Dalkeith Advertiser, about someone burning clothes in a *"suspect's"* home in the Newtongrange, area, possibly Reed Drive, where the burning of clothes and other evidence from poaching, and other criminal activity, was not unusual. The very house where John Ferris and Gordon Dickie went immediately after they left the murder scene. The same Ferris and Dickie who destroyed their moped, were advised by Alice Walker not to go forward to the police, and one cut his own hair to change his appearance.

Details of a *"female relative"* of the suspect or suspects, who was thought to have burned clothes and was questioned about the fire at the Reed Drive house, were never disclosed to Luke Mitchell's defence team. John Ferris's mom, Catherine, and her daughter, Yvonne, were widely reported as burning clothes soon after the murder on waste ground in Stone Place. This was around 450 metres from the home addresses of Yvonne and

Alice Walker. Despite these addresses being closely linked to three suspects in the murder, upon finding burnt remains the police decided not to follow up the inquiry because the fire was in the "wrong area". The Reed Drive fire, also, was just 400 meters from the gang hut of Joe Jones, John Ferris and Gordon Dickie and the police thought it was the wrong area?

Despite the story of burning clothes being reported only in the local newspaper, Luke Mitchell was asked about this by James Matthews in the Sky TV interview. This leads me to wonder, did the police advise James Matthews about this matter, as its unlikely he ever read the Dalkeith Advertiser?

Luke Mitchell told him straight out, *"It wasn't us",* although regardless of the fact that Reed Drive/Newtongrange was approximately a mile away from Newbattle Abbey Crescent where the Mitchell's lived, by the time the time it got to court it was claimed it WAS them who burned the clothes.

It must be said here, the BBC Institution, Crime Watch, who with the help of the public aided in solving some of Britain's most serious crimes, offered Lothian and Borders Police assistance by suggesting they could carry out a reconstruction of Jodi's movements and highlight the case. Lothian and Borders Police declined.

"Were there any other suspects or people questioned during the police investigation?"

"Several people were questioned extensively by police and ruled out including most of the people mentioned in the documentary.

Mark Kane, who it was alleged was in the area the same time as Jodi and had scratches on his face, was cleared of any involvement by police. His pal Scott Forbes said Kane, a student at Newbattle Abbey College at the time of the murder, had written an essay on `killing* *a girl in the woods` and that a lecturer at the college could confirm this. He added Forbes had told Kane to `play along` "and we will get £50,000 from the newspapers. Kane later died and was totally ruled out as a suspect by police.

The whereabouts of all family members was examined to help develop a timeline of what happened. This is routine during all murder investigations and nobody else was considered a suspect."

As stated earlier, no one trashes your name more than someone who is afraid you will tell the truth.

The claim that, *"several people were questioned extensively"* is, in my opinion, a joke.

In the reporter's submissions she mentions no other suspects, except Mark Kane, and claims *"most"* suspects mentioned in the TV documentary were questioned extensively. What an embarrassment to come out with such nonsense. I have seen the transcripts of the interviews with those people – the only thing they were questioned extensively about was Luke Mitchell. However, it does give an example of how falsehoods were fed to the public throughout the entire investigation.

Records show Mark Kane was living and signing on from Newbattle Abbey College at the time of the murder of Jodi Jones. Hard evidence and several witnesses corroborate this. Many people provided statements that he had scratches on his face and was acting strange in the days after the murder. Several had made the police aware of Mark Kane living in Newbattle Abbey, despite the term being finished.

Mark Kane admitted in his statement that he went to Dalkeith Police station two days after the murder and that police took his name and contact details and said they would be in touch, with note on their files *"to be traced and interviewed"*.

So, we have man in the area the time of the murder, on a cocktail of drugs including methadone, speed, Valium, cannabis *(the drug attributed to the murder of Jodi)* and alcohol, with serious mental health issues, a history of violence, self-harm, drug abuse, cruelty to animals, scratches on his face, and who was a regular visitor to the woods where Jodi was found, attending occult meetings with a group of others with an interest in the supernatural. He was in a police station two days after the brutal murder of Jodi Jones, and the police did not question him until two years later, months after Luke Mitchell had been convicted. Yet according to a hack reporter, he was *"totally ruled out as a suspect by police"*.

Mark Kane told me *"It looks bad, I even wrote an essay on killing a woman in the woods"*. The tutor didn't remember the essay, submitted two years previously, so this *"totally cleared"* Kane of any involvement in the murder of Jodi Jones....this to me about sums up the police "investigation" and the reporting by their friend in the media.

James Falconer, the "condom man" was not questioned by police until three years after the murder despite his DNA being on a condom meters away from where Jodi's body was found. He claimed to have been in the woods at approximately 9 p.m. having a "clean wank," 15 meters away from where the mutilated body of Jodi Jones was lying.

He claimed the time of night he was there was when it was "grey dark". For the last eighteen years, criminologist, Dr Sandra Lean, has examined the light on the 30th of June and timed what time "grey dark" happens. The average time is 10.30 p.m. Alice Walker said when she was on Roan's Dyke Path, after 11 p.m., they didn't always have the torches on as it was light.

Police just accepted that a man walked 500 yards or more from his home to go into the woods to have a "clean wank". The condom found didn't give a reportable result from the outside of the condom, which meant he was either wearing gloves or the condom had been wrongly handled by the police, destroying the DNA on the outside of condom. The sperm inside the condom belonged to James Falconer, yet he wasn't questioned for three years. My investigations told me he was there with an underage {15 year-old} girl, although he claimed to his work mates he was there with a married woman and that's why he couldn't say who he was with. Either way, it's irrelevant when a young girl is murdered.

James Falconer, on the morning of the 1st of July 2003, like everyone else in Dalkeith and Edinburgh woke up to the news that a young girl had been murdered, in the very place where he had been that night. His reaction was to go back out onto Lady Path at the back of Reed Drive and into the woods for another wank.

On the 6th of July 2003, the Sunday Mail wrote,

"The murder team believe there is a growing body of evidence to suggest she {Jodi} interrupted a flasher, peeping tom or someone else committing a sex act. It is now their strongest line of inquiry.

"The attack on Jodi as she walked to Luke's from her home in Easthouses was not planned or premeditated. It was frenzied, rushed and amateurish"

"Jodi was not sexually attacked but the team are working on the theory the killer was a sexual deviant or was committing a sex act. It may or may not have been someone she knew but we believe he was on his own".

"He may have been disturbed by Jodi's arrival or her reaction and attacked her. He just flipped. We are also interested in the fact the killer appears to be someone who habitually carries a knife".

"Detectives initially discounted a sexual motive as there was no evidence of an indecent attack on Jodi. Now they believe the killer was "sexually embarrassed" before he started the attack on the Roan's Dyke pathway between Jodi's home in Easthouses and Luke`s home in Newbattle"

This type of scenario, if it was true, would explain why *"numerous semen deposits"* were found on Jodi's body and clothes. Stephen Kelly's sperm was found on Jodi's T-shirt. In any other murder case, he would have been a prime suspect as a result. Instead, the police handed him an explanation as to how his semen was found on Jodi's T-shirt.

On the 2nd of July 2003 police were in James Falconer's home, after two youths had found a "hoodie" at the back of Reed Drive in the undergrowth at Lady Path. This was where Falconer went for a wank on the day after Jodi was murdered, and an area that was supposed to be secured for forensics. James Falconer's mother claimed the `hoodie` belonged to her son. The boy said that he had given the `hoodie` to his pal a week before and his pal had thrown it away.

Door to door inquiries by the police stopped short of James Falconer's house in Reed Drive and the home of Gordon and David Dickie. No one knows why. Almost three years after Jodi's murder, the DNA found inside the condom was identified as James Falconer's.

John Ferris and Gordon Dickie, who were known to have been close to the murder scene at the very moment of the murder, destroyed evidence, including a moped and clothes, Ferris cut his own hair, and on the instruction of Alice Walker, both men refused to go forward to police until after they had time to concoct a story about their whereabouts on the day of the murder. Police never bothered to check if the moped had indeed been destroyed in the local scrap yard. The police did not investigate the story the two told. Their `extensive questioning` was more to do with Luke Mitchell than their whereabouts.

"The whereabouts of all family members was examined to help develop a timeline of what happened. This is routine during all murder investigations and nobody else was considered a suspect."

On the16th of July 2003, 16 days after Jodi had been murdered, the police made an appeal for a "stocky man" dressed in dark clothing, who had been seen following Jodi on the evening of the murder, to come forward. DI Tom Martin said this was a "significant" breakthrough as it was the first positive sighting of Jodi on the night she was murdered.

Two independent witnesses had seen Jodi walking along Easthouses Road toward Roan's Dyke Path at around 5 p.m. followed closely behind by a man, estimated to be in his 20`s, approximately 5` 10" in height, of stocky build, wearing dark clothing and possibly carrying a backpack.

DI Martin said the sightings were "credible" and an important breakthrough and asked the public to *"search their conscience"* and come forward with the name of the man the police were looking for.

One of the witnesses claimed they had seen the same man a week later at the police reconstruction of Jodi's movements. The man was on Morris Road, Easthouses around 6 p.m. with two other men. This man came forward and was not the man who was seen on the night of the murder. He admitted that he was likely the man in question on the night of the reconstruction, but was not the man following Jodi Jones on the night she was murdered – he was provably nowhere near Easthouses on June 30th.

Nevertheless, on the 19th of July police, through the media, said *"Man at Centre of Jodi Appeal Found"*

This was another lie being spread by the police and media. No real attempt was made by police to find the "stocky man" who was following Jodi Jones, because by that time they had detained Luke Mitchell for questioning two weeks earlier, and through pals in the media, told the public they were not looking for anyone else. While it was widely accepted that the "stocky man" was Joseph Jones, Alan Ovens and Judith Jones said Joseph never left the house that afternoon or evening.

Ten weeks after the murder, one of the witnesses came forward again to say they had seen the "stocky man" again and would be able to pick him out from a crowd of men she did not know. There is no record of police following this up.

Two independent witnesses had seen a stocky man following Jodi and wearing different clothes than what was described by Andrina Bryson at the Easthouses end of Roan's Dyke Path.

Why the police waited until the 16th of July to make the appeal makes no sense, unless they genuinely didn't want to find the "stocky man," as they were by now making a murderer out of schoolboy Luke Mitchell to cover up their incompetence.

By now, the police were only interested in Luke Mitchell, and *"no other suspects"*, while other suspects were being ignored, permitted, and indeed encouraged to lie.

We now have three members of the Jones family who everyone, apart from the police it would seem, believed they could be seen as potential murderers or at least suspects. All three had now refused to *"search their conscience"* and come forward to help police after appeals had been made.

In addition, we have John Ferris and Gordon Dickie, who had been together on the day of Jodi's murder and were at the locus at the time Jodi was being murdered, and we have Joseph Jones, the "stocky man", following his sister and possibly the last person to see her alive. Yet police accepted their lies without investigating them.

We have Alice Walker, Jodi's grandmother, telling John Ferris and Gordon Dickie not to go forward to the police and we had Judith Jones and Alan Ovens lying in order to create an alibi for Joseph Jones, who claimed he never left his home all afternoon and evening.

"What was significant about Jodi`s being discovered by Mitchell and the search party?"

"Mitchell discovered Jodi's body, which was hidden behind a wall on the path, after claiming his dog led him to the scent, Family members with him said he appeared to know where the body was. This contradicted his evidence the dog had led them to the wall. He also showed no emotion at the horrifying sight.

When he was later questioned, he mentioned he had a distinctive hair clasp which was not readily visible on Jodi`s body and his description of her clothing implied he had seen her much later than just at school as he had claimed."

This was nothing more than trash and spin to keep up the creation of `pantomime villains` of the Mitchell family and to con the public, while disrespecting a murder victim.

Luke Mitchell claimed his dog, Mia, reacted at the wall by putting her front paws on the wall and sniffing the air, approximately 20 meters past the V, after telling her to "go find Jodi". He then went back to the break in the wall {V} and climbed over and walked in the direction the dog had indicated. This is where Jodi was found.

Stephen Kelly and Janine Jones both corroborated Luke Mitchell's story about Mia the dog reacting at the wall past the V in their initial statements to the police.

Kelly said the dog was "big" with her front paws on the wall, her head being higher than the V in the wall as she was sniffing the air. Janine Jones said the dog got all excited after they passed the break in the wall. Alice Walker said she didn't see how the dog reacted as she had fallen back a little bit as they walked down the path.

After Luke Mitchell was detained on the 4th of July with full media coverage, with police looking for *"no other suspects",* and the Jones family now openly admitting that they believed it was Luke Mitchell who had killed Jodi, the police went back for several more statements from the search party. Now, according to these revised statements, Luke Mitchell walked straight to the body of Jodi Jones.

"He also showed no emotion at the horrifying sight." This is simply untrue and gives you an idea of the standards and tactics used by the media to paint a horrible picture.

Stephen Kelly, Janine Jones, and Alice Walker all spoke about how *"shocked"* Luke was coming back over the wall after discovering the body. Janine described his eyes, *"wider than normal with shock"* and said there was *"concern in his voice."*

The first policeman on the scene asked Luke Mitchell to go back over the wall with him to show him where Jodi was. *"I'm not going back over there"* came his response, his legs nearly buckling underneath him, as he propped himself up against the wall. The first police on the scene said Luke Mitchell was in shock, scared, frightened, and visibly upset.

But the reporter parrots Dalkeith CID's first impression of Luke Mitchell sometime later at Newbattle school: *"He also showed no emotion at the horrifying sight."* This was a Dalkeith CID officer's hunch and is the sole `evidence` against Luke Mitchell yet spun as `facts`.

When he was later questioned, he mentioned she had a distinctive hair clasp which was not readily visible on Jodi`s body and his description of her clothing implied he had seen her much later than just at school as he had claimed."

Alice Walker approached Jodi's body after both Luke Mitchell and Stephen Kelly had been over the wall. It was originally claimed Mrs Walker "cradled" Jodi's body, although this later changed to "touched her forehead." If Mrs Walker moved Jodi's head, it's impossible to say what Luke Mitchell might have seen – the crime scene photos were taken after three of the four searchers went over the wall.

In an interview with a journalist the word *"scrunchie"* was written down and, in giving evidence, the journalist said that would not be a word he would use to describe a hair clasp so Luke Mitchell must have used that word.

To describe Jodi's clothing from what Luke, Stephen Kelly, and Alice Walker witnessed that night would not be difficult. Her trousers were used to bind her arms/hand, light blue socks on her feet, and the rest of the items were lying on the ground around her body.

There are many things in this case that stick in my mind and puzzle me. After Jodi's body was discovered and the search party were making their way back up the path, Janine Jones, the only one in the party not to see Jodi, asked Stephen Kelly if Jodi had been *"naked"* when she was found.

Janine Jones had tragically experienced her father's suicide by hanging and her brother Joseph allegedly attempted the same. She also knew that Jodi had self-harmed in the past, so my thinking is that when Jodi was found dead, why would she not think hanging, suicide or self-harm? Why would the first question be to ask if she was naked? Did she think someone she knew could have hurt her sister and that that person could strip her?

The first thing I have to say about the search party is that Luke Mitchell was the only male connected to Jodi Jones who cared enough to go out in search of her. It has always puzzled me why no males in the Jones' family went looking for a wee girl reported missing.

Why didn't Joseph Jones and Alan Ovens, who were less than a three-minute walk away from Roan's Dyke Path, where the search party started, offer to assist? Instead, they permitted an old woman and a young girl go out at night into woods/fields to look for Jodi. That doesn't seem right.

In addition, there were John Ferris and Gordon Dickie minutes away from where Jodi was found, who knew the area very well, but never attempted to look for the missing girl. It has been suggested that no one apart from the search party were worried about Jodi being missing as it wasn't uncommon for her to be out late, against orders from her mother.

But there was something different on the night of the 30th of June 2003. Different enough for her sister Janine, her boyfriend Stephen Kelly, and the head of the family, Alice Walker, to leave Mayfield and walk approximately two miles to meet Luke Mitchell to search for Jodi.

It was Alice Walker who headed straight to Roan's Dyke Path, and after meeting Luke Mitchell where Roan's Dyke Path meets Lady Path, it was Alice Walker who insisted they go back down the path where Luke Mitchell had just come, to *"double check"* as Alice Walker put it.

Luke Mitchell didn't try and get out of going back down the path. Instead, he asked if they had anything belonging to Jodi so the dog, Mia, could track her. Alice Walker said if her house wasn't so far away, she would have gone back to get something, however Jodi's house was less than three minutes away so what was to stop them going to her house to get clothes?

It was Alice Walker, Jodi's granny, the same granny who advised John Ferris and Gordon Dickie not to go forward to police when the police were appealing for them to do so, that led the search party to the body and **not** Luke Mitchell.

"What about the used condom found near Jodi`s body"

"Jodi was not sexually assaulted in any way. Mitchell's defence team claimed DNA in the condom belonged to another man-James Falconer-but during an appeal hearing in 2008 Donald Findlay QC, who was Mitchell's lawyer, told the judges he was dropping any further claims about James, who had already been ruled out of any involvement by detectives investigating the case"

To say Jodi Jones *"was not sexually assaulted in anyway"* is totally disrespectful toward Jodi Jones.

Written by a person with no knowledge of what they are writing, or by a person so desperate to protect themselves and friends that they come out with such nonsense every time their work comes into question.

Either way, its shows a total lack of respect for the victim and the nature of the crime. It also provides another example of how some in the media acted in this case.

Imagine a used condom found approximately 15 meters away from a brutal murder and the police are too lazy, inept, or corrupt to care about such evidence and don't ascertain who that condom belonged to for three years.

To add insult to injury, the DNA on the `hoodie` found on Lady Path which wasn't tested, could have identified James Falconer much earlier, or if the police had asked who lived in the house when they interviewed Falconer's brothers and mother, this matter could have been closed much earlier.

For a reporter to dismiss a used condom filled with semen found at a murder scene to cover up the police ineptitude is appalling.

The police, because they didn't find vaginal trauma or wounds which would suggest rape, couldn't make up their minds if sex had been a motivating factor or not.

Yet initially, on 6th July 2003, the police were claiming "*The murder team believe there is a growing body of evidence to suggest she {Jodi} interrupted a flasher, peeping tom or someone else committing a sex act. It is now their strongest line of inquiry.*

"Detectives initially discounted a sexual motive as there was no evidence of an indecent attack on Jodi. Now they believe the killer was "sexually embarrassed" before he started the attack"

Common sense tells you that a used condom at the scene, when you're looking for a flasher or pervert, would be very important to the investigation. Only the police and their hack reporter didn't see the significance.

Jodi Jones was stripped naked, apart from her light blue socks which appear to have come off as she was dragged and later carefully put back on, with her arms tied behind her back. That, in itself, is sexual.

Her murder was described by the FBI as a *"Lust Murder,"* a murder where the killer stabs, cuts or mutilates the sexual parts of the body for sexual pleasure. This is known as Evisceration Piquerism. The removal or mutilation of the breast in the female victim is "de feminization."

A Forensic Medicine Report completed in October 2004 spoke of the *"sexually motivated homicide"* and agreed with the FBI findings that the post-mortem injuries reflected *"piquerism" ..." that is to say, gaining sexual pleasure from cutting and stabbing".*

The report was significant regarding the *"sexual element of the crime."* Professor Anthony Busuttil described Jodi's murder: *"a sexually motivated homicide of a young woman."*

Lust killers aren't satisfied with just the murder, they have to mutilate or use the corpse in a posing fashion. This all fit with the murder of Jodi. To cut the breast away or mutilate it is also an indication of the *"cutting away"* of the relationship with the mother, a `mummy's boy` wanting to free himself.

The FBI reported that Jodi's murder was a lust killing, but because it doesn't fit in with the police or Ms Hamilton's narrative, they just feed the public falsehoods when their incompetency and moral misconduct is highlighted. The FBI are correct when they stated, *"its disrespectful to the victim and is morally wrong".*

"What was Luke's alibi and why didn't the jury believe him?"

Luke Mitchell's alibi was that he was at home cooking dinner when Jodi died on June the 30th 2003.

But his brother, Shane, gave crucial evidence during the trial which cast doubt on this evidence. Luke Mitchell's mother, Corinne, gave evidence that when she returned home from work at 5.15pm he was in the kitchen. In a statement to police on the 7th of^ July 2003, Luke's brother Shane said he recalled seeing Luke in the kitchen "mashing tatties".

But when Shane was questioned by police on 14th April 2004, he said he had been looking at porn on the internet in his bedroom and this was not something he would have done if there had been anyone else in the house at the time. This contradicted what Luke Mitchell and his mother had told the police.

Shane later admitted on the stand he had discussed his earlier statement with his mother before telling police Mitchell had been at home. He admitted that the statement was not accurate. As the alibi was not held up in court, Corinne was arrested for perjury, however prosecutors made a decision not to proceed with the charges.

Again, this is a shocking example of the methods used by hack reporters to create a monster of a child to gain a conviction.

The simple answer as to why the jury didn't believe Luke's alibi is that the jury from Edinburgh had been fed lies, spin, and trash talk, such as sexual relationships with his mother, and that he was "evil", from as early as the 4th of July 2003.

The truth is Luke Mitchell, the supposed criminal master mind who was able to commit a gruesome murder and not leave a thread of forensic evidence behind, didn't really have an alibi. Shane Mitchell was so nonchalant in his first statement about Luke he said he wasn't sure if Luke was in the house or not.

Nevertheless, let us examine the Ms Hamilton's spin and untruths.

"Shane was questioned by police on the 14th of April 2004" ....

Shane Mitchell was driving to his work and came across a roadblock which he believed was road tax checks, however it was a block set for him. He was dragged from the car and put face down on the road, similar to what you see on the television when police are arresting terrorists.

He was questioned as a suspect for perverting the course of justice, charges which were later dropped. His evidence was permitted in court by the trial judge, Nimmo Smith, as the charges had been dropped and the Crown claimed he was being questioned as a witness and not an accused. Otherwise, the evidence obtained through the questioning on 14th April 2004 would have been inadmissible in court.

Corinne Mitchell was arrested on the same day, April 14th, 2004, and also charged with perverting the course of justice. These charges were later spread all over the media, however the charges never materialised (like her son, Shane, the charges were later dropped). When giving evidence, it is common practice for most witnesses in a High Court trial to be warned about the risks and penalty for perjury. This was true for Corinne Mitchell as well. The Crown didn't proceed with perjury charges because there were NO grounds to do so.

This was another slander campaign by the police and fed to their friends in the media. The public then believed that the Mitchell's were are all guilty, making the campaign a success. Around about this time, the rumours in the Dalkeith and Edinburgh area were that Luke Mitchell was taking the blame for his brother Shane, who had a history of being mentally ill and been in Rosslynlee Psychiatric Hospital as a patient, prior to and after the murder of Jodi Jones. Again, these were lies being presented to the public by the media. We now know that it was Jodi's brother, Joseph, who had had a history of mental illness and had been a patient under the Mental Health Act, prior to the murder, after the murder, and at times just prior to the trial of Luke Mitchell.

Discrepancies in witnesses' statements pertaining to an incident years, or even months before, are NOT perjury. A material effect on the outcome of the trial would have to have transpired for perjury to have occurred.

While Corinne Mitchell was on the stand the court was cleared for legal arguments and the charges of perverting the course of justice against Corinne Mitchell were dropped.

And while Shane Mitchell was being dragged from cars by countless police officers, the same police were taking drug dealers and poachers on tours of the locus, allowing lies in a murder investigation, all the while permitting the destruction of evidence to go unchecked.

LIES AND PERJURY

On the 23rd of February 2012 Corinne Mitchell took a Polygraph test, a test which she had requested from day one of the investigation, and while they are inadmissible in a Scottish Court, they nevertheless are used in the criminal justice system. Probation Services carried out tests repeatedly, returning scores of sex offenders back to prison if they failed the test.

They give insight into who is and isn't being truthful and, if coupled with the evidence in the case, both Luke Mitchell and his mother were more than happy to take the test. This is very telling as, if they failed, you could only imagine the backlash from the media.

DS Craig Dobbie and Jane Hamilton should have had to take a polygraph test and asked if they fitted up Luke Mitchell while disregarding all other evidence.

Corinne Mitchell was asked three specific questions of which she was not made aware prior to them being asked:

1) *Did she falsify Luke's` alibi?* Answer: No

2) *Did she burn any clothes or evidence that would have incriminated Luke?* Answer: No

3) *Did she lie in her court testimony?* Answer: No

Test results were: Passed the polygraph test with "No-Deception Detected"

Terry Mullins, in addition to being a leading Polygraph Expert, is a man of integrity, which I witnessed for myself when a professional football player attempted to manipulate his results after taking a test. I have no doubt whatsoever that if he had suspicions about Luke or his mother's test he would have spoken out. Instead, Terry Mullins describes Luke Mitchell as a "victim" and stands by that statement and the results of the mother and son's tests completely.

Bob Smyth, a brave man with integrity, wrote in the Mail on Sunday, "*She was telling the truth.* At long last a positive story about the case and someone not afraid to speak the truth.

Two months later, within Shotts's prison, Luke Mitchell took the first ever polygraph test conducted inside a prison, and in similar fashion was not made aware of the questions that were going to be asked.

1) *Did you stab Jodi?* Answer: No
2) *Were you present when Jodi was stabbed?* Answer: No
3) *Did you know where Jodi body would be found?* Answer: No

Like his mother, Luke Mitchell passed the test with "No Deception Detected."

Terry Mullins concluded: *"I'm certain of the test result. Its absolute. I can't believe that Luke Mitchell was convicted on the evidence presented".*

I heard criticism that Luke Mitchell had in some way "conned the test" because he took it while his eyes were closed as he answered the questions. Shotts' prison agent rooms, where the test was conducted, have glass partitions which people can look through while you're visiting. The last time I had a visit with Luke Mitchell in 2010, the late Martin Hamilton, a Glasgow gangster, was in the next booth and kept looking into where we were meeting. This was very off-putting. When Luke Mitchell took the polygraph test, prison officers were looking in and trying to distract him, so Terry Mullins advised him to close his eyes.

Alice Walker, a woman who had impeded the police investigation from the very beginning, came out and condemned that polygraph test saying, *"it doesn't prove anything, he is a lying cheating murderer."*

Other detractors came out in force claiming the test was nothing more than a *"crass publicity stun*t." An accusation, in my opinion, that was classic projection because that is what the whole case against Luke Mitchell was - *"crass publicity"* peddled by DS Craig Dobbie's friends in the media.

Luke Mitchell knew the polygraph test was inadmissible in Scottish Courts, although the SCCRC do take the findings into consideration as they examine cases. Luke Mitchell did the test because he knew that they could, and did thankfully, change public opinion - the very thing that convicted him. Public opinion that was shaped by lies, spin, and conjecture by the police's spin doctors and friends in the media.

"What about the missing knife?"

"At the time of the murder Mitchell owned a `skunting` knife which has never been found despite an extensive search of his house. During a search of the family home many months later the pouch from the knife was found. Inscription on it read "666" JJ 1989-2003 (Jodi's birth and death)"

First, to imply that this pocketknife could have been the murder weapon is not only preposterous but absolutely shocking and disrespectful to Jodi Jones and the nature of the murder.

The `skunting knife` was a pen knife, with a blade less than 50 mm. Records show the knife was handed in to the police by Luke Mitchell's solicitor, Nigel Beaumont, who gave a statement confirming that.

The *"never been found knife"* was shown to Luke Mitchell in police photographs on the 14th of August 2004.

It was quite comical during the interrogation when the police, while showing him a picture of the knife, asked Luke Mitchell, *"is that your knife."* Luke responded, *"yes, that my fishing knife."* Police asked," *where is it?"* Luke - *"I don't know, you` s have got it, you took photos of it."* Here were police officers with police photographs of a knife that was in their possession asking a boy where it was.

Receipts and credit card statements prove the knife was purchased by Corinne Mitchell from a mail order company in Leeds months after the murder of Jodi. The `missing knife` argument and headlines implied that this knife was a replacement for "the murder weapon" which Luke Mitchell had made "disappear", as he allegedly had with all other evidence.

The facts are the police had a knife taken in an early search, then found a pouch without a knife months later, and Luke Mitchell's lawyer handed the second the knife into the police.

The inscription on the pouch, JJ 1989-2003, represented Jodi's birth and death years and were alongside Jodi's favourite quote, *"The finest day I ever had was when tomorrow never came"*, by Kurt

Cobain. The same quote was on a card left at Jodi's grave, along with flowers, by Luke Mitchell.

The `666` was evidence led in court. The explanation for the 666 was that whoever murdered Jodi was evil and had written alongside her favourite quote.

Nevertheless, it's preposterous to suggest or imply, as the above does, that this knife could have been the weapon used to murder and mutilate Jodi Jones. The defensive wounds on Jodi's body are similar to the wounds I've witnessed in machete attacks. A weapons expert informed Dr Lean that the weapon used was like an `axe type weapon` - a heavy bladed instrument and certainly not a pen knife.

Moreover, pathologist Professor Busuttil said the injuries to the back of Jodi's mouth and throat *{if inflicted through the mouth}* would have had to been caused by a much longer blade, because if a smaller knife had been used there would have been damage to Jodi's teeth and the hands of the murderer. There was no such damage to Jodi's teeth. Luke Mitchell had no injuries to his hands, or anywhere else for that matter. The police had him stripped naked and all his clothes were taken from him on the night of the murder. There were no reports of scratches or injuries of any kind.

"What's the connection with the Black Dahlia murder?"

"Two days after the murder Mitchell bought a Marilyn Manson DVD, "The Golden Age of the Grotesque," which included images of a naked women tied together and subjected to a form of abduction.

Manson had an exhibition of the same name published on his web site, which included images depicting the death of the actress, Elizabeth Short, also known as the "The Black Dahlia", who was mutilated and murdered in Los Angeles in 1947.

Professor Anthony Busuttil, the pathologist who examined Jodi's body, gave evidence that while not identical, there was some similarity between the location and the injuries inflicted on Jodi and those on the actress."

The Black Dahlia murder has similarities to the murder of Jodi Jones as both victims were white females and both bodies were mutilated...there end the similarities.

It certainly wasn't a copycat murder. The similarities between the two murders were, according to Professor A Busuttil, *"aside from the fact that they were both apparently sexually motivated homicides of young women with post-mortem mutilations of the body with a sharp instrumen*t" there were, *"No forensically significant similarities between the injury patterns in these two victims"*

A Goth who buys a music magazine, which includes a promotional Goth Rock Stars DVD and an out-of-date calendar of the rock star, led to speculation that Luke Mitchell was *"obsessed"* with Marilyn Manson. Janine Jones was massively into Marilyn Manson and owned every CD and DVD but it didn't make her the killer. I can assure you that the injuries inflicted on Jodi Jones have more in common with Jack the Ripper's victims than Elizabeth Short.

All that aside, living a few hundred yards away from Luke Mitchell was Mark Kane, a drug addict with a real obsession with mutilated corpses. His closest friends said in the days after the murder, the level of depravity in the websites he visited increased massively. Marilyn Manson was mild in comparison.

Maybe more importantly, Jodi Jones' injuries were as similar to that of wildlife crimes and the mutilation of animals, which wildlife police officers find regularly. They were more in common with the injuries of mutilated deer than that of Elizabeth Short.

"What is the significance of the speaking clock phone call?"

At 16:54 Mitchell made a call to the speaking clock from his mobile. When asked by police why he had called the service when presumably he was in the house as his alibi claimed and there would be other ways to find out the time such as a clock on the wall, he said he couldn't answer why he made the call.

This piece of evidence backs up the prosecution case that he was on his way to meet Jodi at their prearranged time.

I genuinely don't see any significance in this call. Luke Mitchell's phone records show he was a regular user of the speaking clock and it was *"just something he did"*. His mobile phone's screen was smashed and prevented him from seeing the time, and the home-made clock in his mother's kitchen was always wrong.

Phone records show he used the service eighteen times in the previous month. Moreover 16:54 is the time Ms Bryson claims to have seen him arguing with Jodi.

MOTHERS AND SONS

The relationship between a mother and her son is a special one. An examination of any prison visiting room will testify to that. They are full of mothers visiting their sons, who can do no wrong in their eyes. It is always someone else's fault that their boy is in prison. A lot admit that they blame themselves, and it is guilt which drives them to visit.

In this case the relationship between the mother and son and how far a mother will go to protect her son is brought into question. Mothers who wanted to protect their son would do anything within their power to save them from harm.

From my own experiences over the years, I've witnessed many mothers, mine included, who would cover for their son when they were in trouble. But to lie for a son who had brutally murdered a wee girl, his girlfriend, would be taking the protection to an altogether different level.

It was alleged by the media that Luke's mother, Corinne Mitchell, lied to police and destroyed evidence to protect her son after the police accused him of murdering Jodi,his fourteen-year-old girlfriend.

At first instance I didn't think a mother would protect her son for such a heinous crime however, over the years, I've asked dozens of mothers if they would protect their son in such a horrific case as the murder of a young girl. Only a minority said they would turn their son in for such a crime if they thought he had committed it. The majority said they would protect their son. I was taken aback by how many said they would protect their son at all costs and would have done anything to prevent him harm. Going to jail for life was serious harm. The nature of the crime was apparently irrelevant.

In 2013 Corinne took a lie detector, or polygraph test whereby she was asked three specific questions which she was not made aware of prior to them being asked.

1) *Did she falsify Luke's alibi?* Answer: NO

2) *Did she burn any clothes or evidence which would have incriminated Luke?* Answer: NO

3) *Did she lie in her court testimony?* Answer: NO

Corinne passed the polygraph test with "No-Deception Detected".

The only thing Corinne possibly did wrong was to put pressure on her other son, Shane, to give a better and more detailed account of his whereabouts in relation to his brother on the 30th of June 2003, after he had given a nonchalant "nothing to hide" statement to the police on the 1st of July 2003. Of course, she did this to assist Luke.

If Corinne Mitchell was alleged to have covered up for Luke, could the same not be said of the mothers of Joseph Jones, John Ferris, Gordon Dickie, James Falconer and Mark Kane?

James Falconer's mother jumped to his defence after a used condom at the locus was found to belong to him. In addition to Falconer lying about the condom, and without knowing any of the facts, his mother, Ann, said: *"I know my son has done nothing wrong. He didn't have anything to do with the murder".*

Helen Dickie, Gordon's mother, had been lying and covering up for her son for years for all sorts of things, and she helped cover for her son and John Ferris when they turned up at her house on the day Jodi was murdered, after leaving the murder scene.

John Ferris's mother covered and supported his drug dealing and had lied for him for years prior to the murder of Jodi.

Judith Jones openly admitted that she lied and covered for her son, Joseph, and the question remains how far she was prepared to go to protect him. I know from statements of others that Judith went to great lengths not to discuss Joseph with police in the immediate days after the murder of Jodi. Her statements became very detailed indeed after the "stocky man" was brought to the attention of the police. These details provided an alibi for Joseph - whether that was because she knew Joseph was the stocky man, or that he had murdered Jodi, remains to be seen.

Mark Kane's mother had been lying and protecting Mark since an early age, after he became the sole male in the home and a heroin addict at age fourteen. She had gone so far as to protect her son at the cost of a family split after Mark had attacked his grandmother for money for heroin. She would have said and done anything for her son. Norma had been lying and covering up for her son since an early age and now lied to the papers claiming her son wasn't at Newbattle Abbey College when Jodi was murdered, and that he was clean of drugs at the time. Norma had protected Mark so much that the family split as a result.

While the mother/son relationship was under scrutiny, there was truly little attention paid to the father/son relationship, mainly because most of the fathers were not in the picture. Except for David and Gordon Dickie. David being the mentor, sharing knowledge, experiences, and protection. On the day Jodi was murdered we know that David Dickie visited the locus soon after his son, Gordon, had left, which was exactly the time of death for Jodi.

MOTIVE

The motive, like every other thing in this case, was never established because, like the rest of the investigation, the police failed to look into any matter unless it involved Luke Mitchell.

The press were asking, *"was the murder planned or the result of an argument", "did it happen because she refused to have sex with him"*, was it because of *"goth subculture, satanism or his chronic cannabis abuse"*, or *"was the killing rooted in the upheaval of his early years, the breakup of his parent's marriage when he was aged 10", "Living out a sick fantasy to replicate the murder of Elizabeth Short"*

Despite one of the largest police operations ever carried out by Lothian and Borders Police, they had provided NO answers, no forensic links to the murder, nothing at all, and that includes motive.

Looking at the horrific injuries inflicted on Jodi Jones and thereafter being asked to believe that these injuries were inflicted as a result of two fourteen-year-olds possibly, maybe, arguing about him having another girlfriend is totally absurd, and anyone with even an ounce of common sense surely cannot accept that as the motive which led to such a brutal killing.

From the outset police claimed that the killer could be someone who was *"sexually embarrassed"*, someone who Jodi had disturbed in the woods committing a sexual act and was embarrassed upon being found out. Police suggested this led to the murder of Jodi.

James Falconer fit that bill and should have been, at the very least, a person of interest to be traced. Police didn't bother to investigate who the condom belonged to which was found fifteen meters away from the locus and site of the murder.

In the BBC Disclosure documentary on the murder case of Emma Caldwell, investigative journalist Sam Poling, explained that street workers who didn't trust, or felt threatened by the man they were with, often left the condom as evidence in case anything went wrong.

Police were too lazy or incompetent to seek out the owner of the condom at the locus to at least eliminate him. A huge oversight, in my opinion, considering their proposed motive of being *"sexually embarrassed"*.

Moreover, with Stephen Kelly's sperm being found on Jodi t-shirt, some reached the conclusion that it was Jodi's sister, Janine who had murdered Jodi after catching her having sex with her fiancée. This was something that I never bought into.

However, the fact police were treating Jodi's murder as a 'sex crime' and asking most of the males involved in the case (including David Dickie) about any sexual advances towards Jodi, it was a line of inquiry that the police should have followed, rather than providing an 'excuse' to Kelly.

Throughout this case there were accusations of incest, mainly directed at the Mitchell family by the police-controlled media. This was solely based on a television interview and a single interpretation of how Luke and his mother had acted throughout the interview.

Yet my own investigation, I found cousins in relationships, John Ferris was allegedly the father of his half-sister Yvonne's child, and none of this was ever examined. The thing that always stuck out for me, was Janine Jones asking Stephen Kelly if Jodi was naked when he found her. That puzzled me and adding to the fact that Janine had left home at fourteen, as Jodi was planning to do at the same age, only added to the questions that were sadly never answered.

Instead, every possible motive was dismissed and never investigated in favour of a possible "tiff" between teenagers.

PSYCHOLOGICAL PROFILING

To establish a motive, it is essential to understand the backgrounds of the persons of interest to ascertain if the motive fits within their characteristics.

Psychological profiling in criminal investigations is also called criminal profiling, used by law enforcement agencies to identify the characteristics, physical traits, occupation, medical history, last activities, marital status, educational development, psychosexual history, and demography of alleged offenders in homicides, sex crimes and terrorism.

The basic theory is that the crime reflects the personality and characteristics of the offender. While two studies have found the science too inaccurate, several studies have found that predictions made by profilers were approximately 66% accurate.

Lothian and Borders police certainly considered psychological profiling valid enough for the two senior officers, Detective Inspector Tom Martin, and the senior detective in the case, Detective Superintendent Dobbie, to fly to the USA in order that the FBI could carry out such profiling of the murderer of Jodi Jones.

It is impossible to read the report on the profile of Jodi Jones' murderer as it has been so heavily redacted. It has been basically rendered useless, with big black marker taken over 90% of the report. Tens of thousands of pounds of taxpayers' money totally wasted on a police jolly to the USA.

The report should have identified, or at least given a detailed description of the killer such as his age, psychological make up, background history, among others, and could have helped to rule people in or out.

Instead of the FBI report helping to identify a possible killer, it identified no-one. All those funds spent on part of an investigation and yet police didn't use it and, similar to the crime scene, destroyed it with a black marker. Why? The most likely reason was because it did not fit the profile of Luke Mitchell.

At the time of reading the report I believed the trip to USA was an exercise in covering up bad police work, to make it appear the police had no left no stone uncovered in their investigation. The FBI report and profiling officers were convinced that it was NOT Luke Mitchell who had murdered Jodi Jones and had strongly advised Lothian and Borders Police of that fact. As that did not that did not suit their narrative however, they simply destroyed the report, covering up its findings. The first thing I would have done as a defence lawyer would have been to get another report done. Unfortunately, that never happened.

Mark Safarik is one of the most respected members of the FBI's elite Behavioural Analysis Unit and an established internationally recognized expert in analysis and interpretation of violent criminal behaviour. Mr. Safarik believed that Luke Mitchell was too young to have carried out the murder of Jodi Jones. He stated that the FBI had carried out *"a detailed profile report"* and Luke was not the killer. *"If you have mutilation of sexual body parts, you are talking about a lust killer and that is not what you are going to find in a boy of 14. The fantasy development and all that dynamic would just not exist at that age".*

Mr Mark Safarik said that DS Dobbie and DI Martin had requested a "fresh pair of eyes" to look at the case and, instead of looking at what direction their investigation was taking, when the report didn't match their theory, they simply ignored the FBI report and advice. He goes on to express that Luke Mitchell is wrongfully convicted and that Lothian and Borders police, led by DS Dobbie, had disrespected Jodi Jones and the Scottish Justice System. He stated that if the police just *"charge someone convenient and who you think you can convict, that's disgraceful"*. Mr Safarik argued that the police actions in this case were a *"disservice to the victim, the justice system and it is morally wrong"* and stated the real killer *"is still out there"*.

The very nature of the brutal murder of Jodi Jones put emphasis of the psychological makeup of the killer. As Mark Safarik stated, the murder and the mutilation of the body could only have been carried out by some deranged psychotic person. Someone evil.

CREATING A MONSTER

Psychological profiling was nevertheless used to smear Luke Mitchell prior to the trial. What the police didn't have on him, they invented, and thereafter put out into the public domain through their hack reporters.

The media interest was intense and for twenty-four hours a day, seven days a week, the Mitchell family was targeted. Their house was under siege, they were followed to work and school, all their neighbours, work colleagues, and school friends were harassed. As a result, and soon after the murder, the recently traumatised Corinne and Luke Mitchell agreed to give an interview to give an interview to Sky TV.

Solicitor Jim Kelly said that the family's lawyer, Nigel Beaumont, should have strongly advised against it, but he was aware that when the family looked for advice, Nigel was often inebriated and incapable. He would call up the Mitchell's late at night after drinking, talking nonsense. He was known to tell some of Edinburgh's criminals that Mitchell was 100% innocent while telling others that Luke Mitchell was a "duplicitous little bastard". What chance did Luke Mitchell have with such a man as his lawyer?

The Sky interview, watched by millions, showed a glassy eyed boy being comforted by his mother. This was misconstrued by the media that there was an unnatural relationship between the mother and son. The public were then led to believe he was having sex with his mother merely because she was showing affection to her son during an unimaginable moment. They published things which created myths in the local area such as, *"he was shagging his ma", she was covering up for him", did you see the evil eyes and stare".*

James Matthews of Sky who conducted the interview with Luke and Corinne Mitchell said:

"It was a time in the murder investigation when detectives had precious little evidence. The findings of Prof. Ekman kept the focus of the inquiry on Mitchell" Very convenient for the police that a journalist would ask questions the police would have liked to ask. Nevertheless, precious little or NO evidence whatsoever renamed the case.

Professor Ekman, known as the "human lie detector" who, based on a pseudo-Science micro expressions, believed that Luke Mitchell was enjoying the interview and fooling the people who watched it into believing he was innocent.

I'm not a professor of a pseudo-science, but with over forty years in the criminal justice system, including serious crime, prison system, and criminal cases, what I witnessed was a ` wide eyed boy ` , frightened, heavily medicated *(which I found to be the case later),* under a great deal of stress, wrongly turning to the media for some kind of help to escape the pressure.

Dr Ian Stephens, a Scottish psychologist who was later accused of sexually assaulting a young patient and who I regret ever working with at the Miscarriage of Justice Organisation, went on TV and declared it was just a *"hunch",* but the way Corinne had been cuddling her son was *"unnatural".* Watching the interview back now, I see two terrified people being questioned by a man who was in all but name a police officer.

Moreover, after the conviction, without ever examining case papers or considering the evidence while a director of an organisation that fights Miscarriages of Justices, Dr. Ian Stephens went on to call Luke Mitchell an intelligent *"loner"*, who had *"unusual circumstances"* in his family life. He went on to compare Luke Mitchell with the Mary Bell {1968} case, who aided police in the search for her victims. Again, without any consideration of case files or consultations, he concurred 100% with the police theory and media narrative that Luke Mitchell had brought forth his own *"downfall"* when he made the *"mistake"* to *"join the search for Jodi and then to find her at a place that nobody else had thought to look".* This could also describe Gordon Dickie, John Ferris, David Dickie, and Alice Walker.

When Dr Ian Stephens was challenged and made aware of another possible suspect, Mark Kane, he looked like a rabbit in the headlights, completely thrown from his train of thought, and stated that Kane would *"certainly be a person of interest"* after he learnt only a fraction of his past.

On the 4th of July 2003, while Luke Mitchell was being interrogated *{a term accepted by the appeal court},* Dr Ian Stephens, in an interview with The Scotsman, could have been describing Joseph Jones, Gordon Dickie or John Ferris, when he said it would be *"unusual for the killer and the victim not to know each other"* and police will focus their inquiry on people *"close to her".*

Dr Stephens could also have easily been describing Joseph Jones, Gordon Dickie, and Mark Kane when he said the killer would *"be someone full of anger".* A person who was likely to be *"a white male under 30 and lives in the local community which explains his knowledge of the pathways"* Ferris, Dickie, Joseph Jones, and Mark Kane knew the locus as a `gang hut` and Luke Mitchell knew the pathways.

Dr Stephens went on to say, that police should be looking for *"people with a record of violence whether its household pets or people.* This certainly ruled out Luke Mitchell, but again described Joseph Jones, Mark Kane, and Gordon Dickie.

Arguments put forward were that because Luke's father had left the family home when Luke was young, he had to take on the position as head of the family, giving a false sense of power at an early age which ultimately led to him having sex with his mother and killing Jodi Jones.

This theory makes absolutely no sense as Luke was the younger brother of Shane Mitchell. Shane would have taken on this role in the family and not Luke. This then led to rumours in the local and surrounding areas, that it was indeed Shane Mitchell who was the killer and that he had been under mental health care for some years in the Rosslynlee Psychiatric Hospital. It was suggested that Luke was taking the fall for his brother. What a load of nonsense but summed up the case and the public perception with regard Luke Mitchell and the Mitchell family.

This rumour that Luke Mitchell was somehow taking the blame for his older brother Shane was encouraged and given believability in the local area by Judith Jones, who claimed Corinne Mitchell was protecting *"her first born".*

As soon as I read Judith Jones' statement my initial thought was classic projection: *unconsciously taking unwanted emotions or traits, behaviour you don't like about yourself and attributing them to someone else.* A common and classic example is a cheating partner who is always accusing their partner of doing what they are doing themselves.

The first born son, taking over the household as head man after the father had left the home, either by splitting from the mother or death, could be attributed to Mark Kane, Joseph Jones, and

John Ferris, but not Luke Mitchell.

The psychological relationship between Luke and his mother, Corinne, was an integral and important part of the Crown's case. It was argued that Corinne, because she had lied to a tattooist in order that Luke could get a tattoo, would be prepared to cover up for him in the brutal murder of his girlfriend.

The jump from a white lie to a tattooist to lying to police in a murder investigation, burning clothes, and destroying evidence was, in my opinion, an incredible leap, but nonetheless believed by the jury. Charges which were brought against Corinne Mitchell and splashed all over the tabloids were ultimately dropped.

The "fact" Luke Mitchell was a Goth, into the music of Marilyn Manson (he owned one CD), and had a fascination with the Black Dahlia murder was based on one music magazine which featured Marilyn Manson, a Goth Rocker who has a painting of the Elizabeth Short murder.

The resemblance of Elizabeth Short's body and that of the body of Jodi Jones became a significant factor in the Crown's case as both corpses had been mutilated. While I found the whole argument about Goth culture and Marilyn Manson bizarre, I could see some resemblance between the two murder victims and in particular, the wounds to the face and head. Yet, I failed to see any real evidence that linked Luke Mitchell to any fascination of the murder of Elizabeth Short or Marilyn Manson for that matter.

CANNABIS RESIN

Cannabis resin was a major contributing factor in the murder of Jodi Jones according to Lord Nimmo Smith who, in sentencing Luke Mitchell, said there was *"no doubt in his mind"* that smoking cannabis resin had led to the psychosis which led Luke Mitchell to murder Jodi Jones, and that smoking cannabis had let to Luke not recognizing *"right from wrong"*. Then there was the claimed fact that Luke Mitchell was a known hash dealer, supplying Jodi Jones and others. There was not a thread of evidence to suggest that Luke Mitchell was in any way mentally damaged by smoking cannabis resin. Lord Nimmo was more accurately describing Joseph Jones, apparently without knowing it.

Joseph Jones was frequently psychotic, paranoid, and violent when smoking cannabis resin. You could be forgiven for thinking Lord Nimmo Smith was describing Joseph Jones rather than Luke Mitchell in his deliberations. But police were only interested in Luke Mitchell's cannabis resin use.

However, within the investigation we have Mark Kane at Newbattle, who sold and smoked cannabis, buying it in the local area. We have John Ferris, Gordon Dickie, and Joseph Jones all selling and smoking cannabis.

At the time in 2003, all suspects or persons of interest were smoking/selling cannabis resin and in particular, soap bar cannabis, which is as hard as a rock. To cut it, you first have to heat it up to make it softer. This requires a sharp knife. Mark Kane, Ferris, Dickie, and Joseph Jones all carried knives for said purpose, although it has to be said Joseph Jones carried a large bowie knife in a backpack for reassurance when he left his home.

SEXUAL EMBARRASSMENT

The worst insult I read in this case was that Luke and his mother, Corinne, were having an *"unnatural relationship"*. In my nineteen years involvement in the case, I never once discovered any evidence to suggest that Luke Mitchell was having an incestuous relationship with his mother. I also found no history of abuse towards animals.

At worst, he was a petulant, arrogant teenager, into goth, smoked weed, and carried a pen knife, which was hardly out of the ordinary for Dalkeith. The mother and son relationship, drug taking, and the psychology of other suspects and people of interest in the case were never heard by the court, the jury, the public, or indeed never investigated by police.

James Falconer, whose DNA/sperm was found in a condom fifteen meters away from where Jodi's body was found, lived a few doors away from David Dickie at Reed Drive and claimed that the condom was at the locus because he had walked down Roan's Dyke Path and into the woods to have a "clean wank". From where he lives in Reed Drive it would be much easier to have taken the same route as David Dickie and the first police on the scene, and I've personally never heard of men going into woods to masturbate into a condom.

His explanation lacked any credibility and many parts of it were proven to be false. Yet when questioned, Falconer claimed he had been questioned by police and *"cleared"* of any involvement in the murder of Jodi Jones. He went on to say, *"we all know Luke did it"* and complained the case had been hanging over Dalkeith for years.

His mother, as if right on cue, defended her son, despite not knowing any of the facts or indeed what her son had been up to the day Jodi Jones was murdered by saying, *"I know my son has done nothing wrong and he didn't have anything to do with the murder".*

The story that he walked 500 metres to have a `clean wank` in the woods which just happened to be fifteen meters from where Jodi Jones was murdered was false.

My investigations led me to believe that James Falconer was at the locus, in a gang hut regularly used by locals with an underage (15-year-old) girl having sex, and as a result of not being able to say who he was with, invented the "clean wank" story. This story changed over time to him having sex with a married woman and he couldn't say who it was.

So here we have a man capable of having alleged sex with a girl around the age of Jodi Jones, and he was prepared to lie despite the seriousness of the murder of a child. We also have his mother prepared to fully defend her son without knowing the facts.

More importantly, on the 6th of July 2003, police stated they were looking for looking for exactly what James Falconer was claiming to be:

"The murder team believe there is a growing body of evidence to suggest she, {Jodi}, interrupted a flasher, peeping tom or someone else committing a sex act. It is now their strongest line of inquiry.

"Jodi was not sexually attacked but the team are working on the theory the killer is a sexual deviant or was committing a sex act. It may or may not have been someone she knew but we believe he was

on his own".

"He may have been disturbed by Jodi's arrival {at the gang hut} or her reaction and attacked her. He just flipped"

Again, this raises the question, which was never asked, what were the "moped boys" doing behind that wall on the 30th of June 2003?

When incestuous behaviour was attributed to Luke Mitchell and his mother, and the incestuous nature of the others in the investigation went unnoticed or not investigated, it surprised me.

Most of the people in the case pointing the finger at Luke Mitchell were all related in some way: cousins, half cousins, married to cousins.

Yvonne Walker, the granddaughter of Alice Walker, is the half-sister of John Ferris, who is reported to be the father of her child. It was a minefield of incestuous relations, with Alice Walker being the common denominator and matriarch. There is a `joke` in and around Dalkeith about the incest that goes on, particularly on Reed Drive and Easthouses.

Reed Drive in Dalkeith is central to this investigation. The police, upon hearing a child was missing, automatically went to Reed Drive and walked across the field from where David Dickie's house was. Reed Drive was also the home of James Falconer, Gordon {19}, and David Dickie {50}, both of whom were questioned about their sexual approaches made to Jodi Jones. A great deal of sexual embarrassment was potential in this case but none of the lines of inquiry were ever followed up.

Jodi was battered black and blue, bludgeoned twice over the

head, and strangled unconscious before she was mutilated and murdered. Gordon Dickie was facing charges for assaulting a woman causing her severe injury with an iron bar. This was prior to the murder of Jodi, but again he was never treated as a suspect.

LIARS

John Ferris and Gordon Dickie, the alleged "moped boys", were both related to Jodi Jones and were at the murder scene at the very time the Crown claimed Jodi Jones was being brutally murdered. They were only meters away and while they claimed neither saw nor heard anything, they were scheming enough to scrap a moped that they had been using that day and which had been parked up against the V in the wall at the time of the murder. In doing so they destroyed any possibility of linking the moped to the murder.

Both suspects were seeped in the culture of poaching, killing and torturing animals and both were experienced in the art of avoiding detection by police and gamekeepers. They were also scheming enough to conspire against Luke Mitchell prior to going forward to the police.

Both John and Gordon went to the matriarch of the family, Alice Walker, for advice after the police made an appeal for anyone who had been in the vicinity of the path that night to come forward. Alice Walker, despite finding her granddaughter's mutilated dead body, told both boys not to go to the police. This hampered the police investigation and gave the boys time to destroy evidence and concoct a story. John Ferris cut his own hair to change his appearance, their mothers and family members burnt clothes on the night of the murder.

Judith Jones even admitted she had never trusted Ferris and that he knew more than he was letting on. Again, when read this I took it to be classic transference.

Mark Kane, or Mark Taylor as he was also known, was from the Gracemount area in Edinburgh and originally from Leith. His father was a violent man who had left the family home when Mark was very young, approximately 10 years old, and Mark took over as head of the house.

Everything the Crown argued against Luke Mitchell such as taste in music, lifestyle, dominating his mother, and carrying a knife could be attributed to Mark Kane tenfold, before adding cruelty and torture of animals, self-harm, history of violence against women, and an obsession and fascination for mutilated corpses.

Mark Kane/Taylor always carried a large knife with him. When I first met him at Newbattle Abbey College he had six-inch blade with him, and I never once saw him without it. When I visited his mother's home with him, I noticed straight away the two female dogs were terrified of him as they hid and cowered away. I believed at the time that they had taken a dislike to him when he had been messed up on drugs.

After the murder of Jodi Jones, I was contacted by school friends of Mark to ask me if he had still been at Newbattle Abbey when Jodi had been murdered. According to school pals, upon hearing about the murder, they had concluded that he was involved. They based their assumption on knowledge of his past behaviour.

Mark Kane had been a serious torturer of animals. The stories I had been told by people who attended school with him were very disturbing. They told me he was known to cut them up and burn them alive, and he took the eyes out of rabbits leaving them blind. Pupils at school stayed away from him and it must be stated that Liberton High School is anything but soft, posh, or short of dangerous and wild laddies, yet Mark Kane stood out as a classmate to avoid.

Acts of cruelty to animals are not merely indications of a minor personality flaw in the abuse, but are symptomatic of a deep, mentally disturbed personality. Research in both in criminology and psychology has established that people who commit acts of violence or cruelty to animals don't tend to stop there. Many move on to their fellow humans.

A study showed that 100% of sexual homicide offenders examined had a history of animal cruelty. This trait is a red flag in the backgrounds of rapists, murderers, and serial killers. According to the Robert Ressler, psychological profiler for the F.B.I., *"these are kids who never learned it's wrong to poke out a puppy's eyes".* Yet Lothian and Borders Police overlooked this characteristic in several possible suspects, including Joseph Jones, Mark Kane, John Ferris, Gordon and David Dickie.

Hearing these stories reminded me of Mark telling me about how he enjoyed watching the eyes of rabbits with the myxomatosis, a highly infectious and usually fatal viral disease of rabbits, causing swelling of the mucous membranes and inflammation and discharge around the eyes. He believed the eyes were the "art" of the disease and showed the inner suffering. At the time I believed it was a comment made to shock, as he liked to do.

Mark, during his time at Newbattle, showed me the self-scarring on his upper torso. He called it "using his body as a canvas". The scarring on his body was hypertrophic, which normally occurs after skin trauma. His arms, legs, and upper body were covered in them.

The injuries to Jodi's face and in particular her eyes, immediately brought to mind Mark Kane's comments about rabbits' eyes being the art displaying the suffering. Sometime later in a meeting at the Forensic Institute in Glasgow, it was said that after killing Jodi, the murderer had used her body as a `*painter would use a canvas*`. The killer had, in his own way, reflected his personality and personal psychosis on to Jodi Jones. This was something that Mark Kane would argue in class and totally comprehend.

Mark Kane had an unhealthy obsession with mutilated corpses and was addicted to web sites showing them. While at Newbattle College he would fall asleep in front of the computer with these images on the screen and other students would complain. He got banned from using the computers at college as result. The images he looked at daily were every bit and worse as the Black Dahlia murder images.

After Jodi's murder his pals said his liking for such images got worse and more extreme; *"it was like he was trying to make us think it was him that murdered Jodi Jones"*, they told me. Sex with corpses were now the sites he visited daily.

Joseph Jones was the number one suspect for those following the case. Sadly, Lothian and Borders Police, and DS Dobbie's team did not investigate him, for reasons only DS Dobbie could answer.

In the days after the murder, locals who knew Joseph personally and by reputation were telling people *"Joseph has gone and done it now"*.

Locals to the Dalkeith area, the stock car racing community, and members of his own family were convinced Joseph had murdered his sister. Despite this, I could find no investigation or questioning of him in the case papers. Confirmation of his name, address and relationship to Jodi was given in the early hours of the 1st of July 2003. There is no confirmation if he gave these details himself, or if someone else gave them when asked who else stayed in the house. There is NO mention of him in statements from Judith, Alice Walker, or anyone else, and it's not until the 5th of July that he was spoken to by police.

Joseph fits the very psychological description given for Luke Mitchell by psychologists and Lord Nimmo Smith QC. He had a history of mental health issues, he was psychotic, had a history of violence toward female members of his family, including Jodi and his mother, and stepfather, Alan Ovens. Moreover, he had a history of violence and cruelty to animals.

As a teenager Joseph Jones found his father in the garden, who had committed suicide by hanging himself. It was reported that Joseph was never the same again, and that he partly blamed his sister for his father's suicide. The night before Mr. Jones hung himself, a nine-year-old Jodi had walked into an "adult party" in the living room of her house. She ran out of the room, grabbing a large bottle of vodka in protest. The following morning Joseph found his father in the garden. His uncle followed his father and committed suicide a year and a day after Jodi was murdered.

We cannot ascertain if Joseph was psychotic prior to his father's suicide, or the psychosis came later, but it can be reasonably assumed that this was deeply traumatising for a teenage boy.

Records show that Joseph Jones had physiocratic episodes brought on by his psychosis, which was exacerbated when he smoked cannabis resin. The very characteristics that Lord Nimmo Smith QC had attributed to Luke Mitchell. He was prone to violent episodes when he smoked cannabis and, on the day of the murder, he had purchased a large slab of cannabis, possibly from Gordon Dickie and John Ferris.

After his father's suicide, through pure fear, violence and intimidation, Joseph became head of the Jones' household and family. He scared them all, including John Ferris and Gordon Dickie, and more importantly Jodi and her sister Janine. He admitted to being sectioned under the Mental Health Act after previously attacking his sister – there has never been any confirmation of which sister.

As a result, we know on the day of the murder of Jodi Jones, there was a very good chance that Joseph was psychotic, brought on by cannabis, a drug he had been warned off many times by his mental health team.

His episodes were frenzied in nature, as was the murder of his sister Jodi. His mother and sisters would leave the house in fear when *"he went off on one"*. It took four and five police officers at a time to calm him down and take him for help. In one episode, he stabbed his mother when she got in between him attempting to stab his friend. He turned up at the home of criminologist, Dr Sandra Lean, and told that her *"that website goes, or you do"*, and then reminded her that he knew where she lived.

On the day of the murder Judith Jones, knowing her son had obtained a large amount cannabis and was smoking a bong {*a device used to smoke cannabis and get a `huge hit`*} up in his room, telephoned the mental health team to cancel his appointment for later that day. She used the usual excuse that the family wouldn't be back in time for the appointment. This came easily to her as it was not uncommon for her to lie to authorities on his behalf.

It is not unusual for violent criminals who are under care of the Mental Health Act to use it as a form of protection from police scrutiny or questioning. They turn up at a psychiatric hospital looking for assistance, and once in care, they have relative protection from police questioning. If police detain a suspect they can, under Sec 14 Criminal Justice Act 1995, question a suspect in their custody. However, if the suspect has voluntarily sought mental health assistance, the police cannot use Sec 14 Criminal Justice Act 1995 and would have to consult with the doctor in charge of the care of the patient before questioning them. Each case is assessed individually. However, a statement taken from a patient under mental health care is inadmissible in court, as the patient is not of sound mind and therefore not capable of giving a statement in law.

Records show that Joseph Jones had been sectioned under the Mental Health Act on two occasions prior to the murder of his sister. On one occasion he was sectioned for attacking his sister.

Six weeks prior to the murder, Joseph had been committed under the Act for eleven days, after crashing up his mother's house and attacking his sister. He was forcefully medicated with Risperidone, an anti-psychotic and schizophrenia drug, with the maximum dosage permitted by law. The effects of the injections last approximately two to four weeks.

On release from the hospital his psychiatrist reported there was "no hope" as Joseph would refuse to take prescribed medication and would continue to abuse cannabis. Therefore, at the time of Jodi's murder, Joseph's medication had worn off and he was heavily indulging in the drug which makes him psychotic.

The psychiatrist continued to say Joseph's home environment wasn't ideal as his mother suffered from an affective disorder and continued to be less than truthful to the psychiatrist when wanting to avoid him, as she did on the day of the murder. I believe there is a very strong possibility that a phone call, cancelling the visit to Jones house from the mental health team on the 30th June 2003, contributed to the murder of Jodi Jones.

After the murder, Joseph Jones is very conspicuous by his absence. Police and others were informed that he was ill due to his sister's murder. He had placed himself out of reach of police questioning. When he was finally questioned, he was heavily sedated, in the company of his mother, who the psychiatric team criticised for lying. He was not smoking cannabis resin as the police were around. A very different Joseph Jones from that on the 30th June 2003. He later used the Mental Health Act on two occasions to excuse himself from giving evidence at the trial of Luke Mitchell. Again, I have to emphasise that this tactic is not unusual for criminals suspected of crimes.

LUKE, AND THE DOGS ATTACHED TO THE CASE

,There was great emphasis on Luke Mitchell's dog, Mia, the German Shepherd who Luke claimed led the search party to the body of Jodi.

Luke stated that while searching for Jodi, when walking down Roan's Dyke Path toward Newbattle, he gave the command to *"find Jodi"* - a fair request for a dog who knows a person well. It's a reasonable assumption to believe a dog would react when coming across a person they know after being told to look for them.

Luke claimed that while searching for Jodi, along with her sister Janine, Stephen Kelly and Alice Walker, Mia started to sniff the air and put her paws on the wall, approximately twenty metres past the V, on Roan's Dyke Path. The V itself would become an intrinsic part of the Crown's case against Luke Mitchell.

All members of the search party confirmed and corroborated Luke Mitchell's description of the events in their original statements. These statements were given while their memories were fresh and with no outside influence.

These statements would later change dramatically after countless conversations about Luke Mitchell within the Jones family, which included suspects Dickie and Ferris, investigating police, and having a journalist friend of the police acting as what some described as a liaison officer between the police and Jones family, claiming Mitchell was the only suspect.

No longer did the search party declare that it was Mia reacting at the wall that led them to Jodi, but instead changed their story to say Luke went straight over the V in the wall and walked directly to where the body was.

Luke Mitchell's version was rejected by the jury and, at a later appeal in 2008, John Beckett QC told the court there was *"no innocent explanation"* for Luke Mitchell finding the body of Jodi Jones. He told the appeal court, *"It is an almost inevitable inference that he knew the body was there, he must have been guilty of murder"*. The defence team did not challenge this. I have to reiterate here that Gordon Dickie and John Ferris knew where to park their moped, close to where Jodi was found. David Dickie knew where to walk and climb over the V in the wall, close to where Jodi was found, and Alice Walker knew what path to go to and then to instruct Luke to go back towards the V, close to where Jodi was found.

MIA

Mia was a young Alsatian dog, eighteen months old, who was undergoing tracking training. Due to Luke Mitchell's claim that it was Mia who led them to Jodi's body, the defence brought an "expert witness" in to test the capabilities of the dog.

These tests were carried out at Scott's Caravan Park in Dalkeith, the Mitchell's family business premises. While the "expert" accepted Mia had received tracking training, he concluded that Mia wasn't an expert tracker.

Being in and around dogs and trainers all my life, I was a little perplexed by why the defence didn't use Mia's actual dog trainer, Jock Pride, a neighbour and friend of the Mitchell family, to carry out these tests. rather than a stranger to the dog.

Anyone who knows dogs will appreciate that dogs react better for those in their "pack". I was further surprised when I read that Jock Pride had not even been on the stand as a witness. In fact, although he was on the Crown's list of witnesses, he wasn't on the defence list.

It was rumoured Jock Pride wasn't called because he was a friend of the Mitchell family and that he had had an affair with Corinne Mitchell, although that was never corroborated or established beyond rumours. More importantly, I failed to see the relevance of how an alleged affair could have any effect on the evidence of a dog trainer in such a serious case.

Around 2011, when we were looking into the case for a fresh appeal, we were contacted by a solicitor who had worked on the case, Jim Kelly. Graham Mann and I met Kelly at a basement cafe in Carlton Place in Glasgow.

I admired his honesty when he said he had been like others and had put his nose in the trough and had been part of an "experiment" with dogs at the locus. He went on to describe how himself, a solicitor from Beaumont and Co., Donald Findlay QC, Findlay's partner Jane Farquharson, and another junior counsel, staged a reconstruction with dogs of all breeds to see how they would react. This was all to be filmed.

Mr Kelly stated, *"the prosecution's case was that Mitchell must have committed the murder because he found the body even though he argued that he had been taken there by his dog"*. Mr Kelly was involved in this reconstruction as he supplied some the working dogs. He went on to say, *"what we set out to do was to show that any dog would have done the same thing as Mitchell had claimed Mia had, which would have cast doubt on the prosecution's claims".*

The idea was that they would take different breeds of dogs into Roan's Dyke Path and the woods where Jodi was found and film how the dogs reacted. The fundamental problem was that no one bothered to bring an animal carcass, which rendered the entire exercise as futile.

Kelly went on to inform us that there were eight people, including a top QC and a film crew, and ten dogs in the woods that day but, *"It was an utter waste of time. I couldn't believe what I was seeing".* They subsequently then retired to the Justinlees pub for a *"jolly"*. This exercise about summed up the defence in the Luke Mitchell trial.

Had the experiment had been carried out correctly *"it could have cast serious doubt on the prosecution's case that Mitchell found the body because he committed the murder".* Not only was the experiment botched, but it highlighted the lack of respect or care afforded to Luke Mitchell and his defence by his legal team.

The Scottish Solicitors Discipline Tribunal has since struck Jim Kelly's name from the Roll of Solicitors in Scotland for unrelated professional misconduct complaints.

Soon after we traced Jock Pride, I called him up and explained we were Luke Mitchell's legal team looking to launch another appeal. He told me in no uncertain terms he wasn't interested in talking to anymore *"parasitical lawyers, and to fuck off".*

How could I argue after what Kelly had told us of an experiment that costs thousands of pounds and the only thing achieved was them having a "jolly" in the pub, as Kelly had put it. Several calls later, after explaining my background and my interest in the case, he agreed to meet me in in Dalkeith.

After introductions I started to tell him about the botched dog experiment and how it failed because no had brought along an animal carcass. He stopped me right in my tracks and said, *"Mia wasn't trained to find animal carcasses; she was trained to find humans".* That was me told.

I asked what his background was and he told me twenty plus years in Royal Veterinary Core, Rank of Sergeant Major, who specialised in German Shepherd dogs, picking them from a young age and dividing them into categories. The not so intelligent dogs were kept for security, more intelligent were trained for finding explosives, and the elite dogs were trained to find both people and explosives. I asked him how good Mia was. *"Exceptional!",* was his immediate reply.

So, we now had an expert at choosing and training German Shepherd dogs, who had trained the dog in question, but had never given evidence. Now who is anyone to question the great QC Donald Findlay, but on this point, anyone could see that it was a huge mistake not to call the actual dog trainer as a witness, given his expertise and his familiarity with Mia. Why the defence did not ask Jock Pride to carry out the experiment they did with their expert witness in Scott's Caravan Park was beyond me as well.

I had noticed during the initial introductions that Jock had some paperwork with him. The paperwork included drawings explaining scent trails, how the scent would lift and climb up the ivy on the wall where Jodi was found, how the scent from Jodi would lift and cling to trees hanging over the wall. I couldn't help but think of Dalkeith Police cutting away tree branches and ivy to take better photographs. He then explained how the dog would have reacted to the scent, with its nose up high at the trees and at the ivy hanging over the wall, standing on its hind legs, front paws on the wall to gain height. The very actions described by Luke Mitchell, Stephen Kelly, and Janine Jones in their original statements.

The logical thing, or the intelligent course of action, would have been to use Mia in a reconstruction of what had transpired on the night Jodi was murdered. Put Jodi's clothes, or a person Mia knew, at the spot where Jodi was found and get someone who was familiar with Mia to order her to go and find the named person or clothes and capture it on film. The perfect scenario, in my opinion, would have been Jodi's clothing and see how the dog reacted to "find Jodi". Luke's legal team, it seems, was too busy having "jollies" to think about an adequate defence for their client.

SPANIELS

The two suspects Gordon Dickie and John Ferris, the boys on the moped, left the murder scene at the exact time the police and Crown say Jodi Jones was murdered, to go to Dickie's father's house on Reed Drive. Gordon Dickie called the police on the 5th of July after his mother told him the police were on the news saying they were looking for him.

Everyone in the local area knew Dickie was at the scene and yet he and Ferris took five days to come forward, giving them time to avoid detection, burn clothes, scrap the moped, Ferris to cut his hair to change his appearance, and come up with a story. When they did come forward, they claimed they had forgotten where they were or who they had seen at the V in the wall.

Dickie and Ferris claimed that soon after they had arrived at his house, David, Gordon's father, had taken nine working spaniel dogs directly across the field at the back of his house to the V in the wall. You must wonder why he would do this? What was he looking for? What had the men on the moped told him? There was no logical explanation why a man would walk across a field directly to where Jodi was found, unless he knew to go there.

We know that the men on the moped left the V in the wall at approximately 5:20 p.m. on the night Jodi was murdered and the short journey to Reed Drive would have placed them there around 5:25 p.m. In his statement, Gordon Dickie confirmed his father left the house to walk the dogs soon after he and Ferris had arrived at his father's home.

Dickie's father walked directly to where Jodi's body was found and had nine working Spaniels with him, yet he claimed not one of the dogs went to a recently murdered corpse approximately twenty meters away. This is unbelievable.

Knowing Spaniel dogs and how they work, I am aware they flush out game in dense brush and undergrowth like where Jodi was found. A recently murdered girl with horrific injuries would have been picked up by the dogs who were less than twenty meters from the V in the wall. Spaniels have an acute sense of smell and can pick up scents, if the air is clear, from distances as far away as twenty kilometres. At twenty metres they would have been all over the corpse.

I could only take three things from this.

The first one is simple. Dave Dickie is a liar and the events he described did not happen, and because he was a 'police asset', taking them on shooting parties and keeping them updated on the local criminals, his excuse was just accepted.

Or he went to the locus to investigate something that had been told to him by his son and Ferris. Upon discovering Jodi's body, he reported back to his son and John Ferris giving them time to destroy evidence and concoct their alibi.

Or the body of Jodi Jones was not at the locus at that time. Meaning Jodi was either murdered at a much later time than determined by the coroner or murdered somewhere else and her body moved to the locus.

David Dickie was an important witness in the murder of a school child, as he was both a corroborating witness for two people of interest in the murder of a child and had been at the murder scene not long after the murder was thought to have occurred. At the very least you would expect that his clothes and boots would be taken to ascertain if they contained any forensics from him or his dogs. Police examined nothing.

Instead of asking questions or carrying out an investigation, Dalkeith Police thought it befitting to engage David Dickie's assistance on or around the 7th of July, two days after his son had come forward.

However, instead of educating police on scent trails, false scent trails, blood spills, decoys, or other detection avoidance methods which he knew well, he went on what can only be described as a mad rant about Luke Mitchell's footprints leading to the Tool Hire shop on Newbattle Road.

After this trip on the 7th of July 2003, a blood like substance was found on the boots of David Dickie. No one could now tell if the substance was connected to the murder and had been picked up on that night, or on the night the police took him to the locus to seek his advice.

The police must have ruled out Ferris and Dickie at this time as they had already informed the media that they, *"weren't looking for anyone else"*, and that there were *"no other suspects"*. The police weren't interested in David Dickie being at the murder scene on the night of the murder and instead of investigating him, they used him as an "expert witness". A man who had previously been at the scene with his dogs and found nothing was suddenly an important witness.

In 2010 I spoke with David Dickie in a field adjacent to Roan's Dyke Path, which was at the back of his house on Reed Drive. I had chapped the door, introduced myself, and asked if he would speak to me, "aye in the field", he said. So, the field it was.

He told me when he took the spaniels over the V in the wall, all except one jumped and as the last one was too old, he had to lift him over. He told me he was a "top dog man and poacher" and that his dogs didn't indicate toward Jodi's body. He claimed, however, that they had picked up the trail of Luke Mitchell on or around the 7th of July and how they had traced his footsteps to the back of the tool hire place on Newbattle Road. He stated that, *"Mitchell was a murdering bastard".*

He couldn't explain to me how such excellent working dogs had missed Jodi. He then finished the interview by telling me, *"And my son won't be talking to you".*

REED DRIVE

Reed Drive is part of a small mining village in Midlothian and is important to the case for several reasons. Firstly, Reed Drive was the home of Gordon Dickie and the house where both he and John Ferris went after leaving the murder scene. They travelled up Roan's Dyke Path, along Lady Path and into David Dickie's home on Reed Drive.

Reed Drive is also the address of James Falconer, the "suspect" who was identified by a used condom found near the murder scene.

Moreover, Reed Drive was the first port of call after Jodi Jones was reported missing.

At the end of Reed Drive, where there is a break in the houses, a matter of twenty yards from the home of David Dickie, you can walk directly in a diagonal fashion across the field adjacent to the locus. The police were at Reed Drive, for what reason (no one knows as it was never investigated), when they received a call that a body had been found. Two uniformed police officers made their way to the locus in the very same footsteps David Dickie had taken earlier with his dogs, the shortest route to the locus.

POLICE DOGS

Police brought in dogs from Strathclyde Police to ascertain if the dogs would act in a similar fashion to Mia. Two dog handlers walked up Roan's Dyke Path, with one climbing over the wall and hiding behind a tree close to where Jodi had been found, while the other walked the dogs past the V in the wall. The dog didn't react and because of this they concluded Mia *"would not have reacted".*

The primary problem with this experiment was that the man on the opposite side of the wall hadn't shed any blood or sweat and hadn't been in a violent struggle fighting for his life. This experiment, in my opinion, was carried out to discredit Luke Mitchell and give the police something to convince Stephen Kelly and Janine Jones that their recollections and statements about how Mia had reacted were wrong.

As you can imagine, on the night Jodi was found Lothian and Borders Police were out in force. What they didn't bring with them, however, were sniffer dogs, despite having them in Dalkeith police station. Strangely, soon after the murder Dalkeith police turned up with dogs for a car break-in to see if they could get the trail of the suspected thief. We have no choice but to conclude that a car theft in Dalkeith warrants the deployment of sniffer dogs, but the murder of a 14-year-old girl does not.

The scent of both the murderer and Jodi would have been fresh and dogs could have possibly ascertained what direction the killer or killers had taken in their escape, or established how Jodi had arrived at the locus.

For several days after, Lothian and Borders Police were talking about bringing in specialist dogs from Yorkshire, so they knew the importance of dogs in this case. Yet they left their own dogs in Dalkeith police station when they were needed most. Another massive failure on behalf of the police.

When they eventually did bring in the dogs from Yorkshire between the 10th and 12th July, the Police had already had David Dickie with his nine spaniels at the locus, obviously prioritising his expertise over that of police trained dog teams. This put paid rest to the press reports that the Yorkshire police team were Lothian and Borders Police *"first port of call."*

The *"cadaver dogs"* were NOT used to ascertain if the dogs would act in a similar fashion to how Mia had reacted to a dead body behind the wall. Instead, the dogs were used to examine *"what direction might the killer have taken"* and in particular had the killer *"escaped towards the Newbattle area...."*

The only routes examined were ones leading to Luke Mitchell's house at Newbattle. From the locus you can walk straight into Newbattle Abbey College, where Mark Kane was living. You can walk straight into Easthouses, where Joseph Jones was across the field on the other side of the wall. You can walk straight to Reed Drive, where Ferris, Dickie, and Falconer all lived. However, none of these routes were checked. This was not an investigation to ascertain answers pertaining to the murder of Jodi Jones, this was an exercise in the hope of helping Police get their boy.

The Yorkshire dog exercise was working off the premise that the killer or killers must have had blood from Jodi on them, or what else could they be following? This put paid rest to the theory that the killer or killers would not necessarily be blood stained as reported.

More importantly the Yorkshire dogs were hampered in their exercise by a *"bleach like substance"*. Before the dogs arrived on July 10th-12th, the murder scene, which was under police control until the 16th of July, had been "bleached".

Only police and criminals know the importance of bleach in destroying DNA. After Jodi was found the site was police protected. Why would the police bleach the murder scene? Or was it the murderer or persons involved in the cover up? Bleach like substances are also used by poachers and gamekeepers to form a 'protected site' and hamper dogs in any search.

PEOPLE

Jodi Jones

Luke Mitchell

Judith Jones

Corinne Mitchell with Dr Sandra Lean

Gordon & David Dickie

Joseph Jones

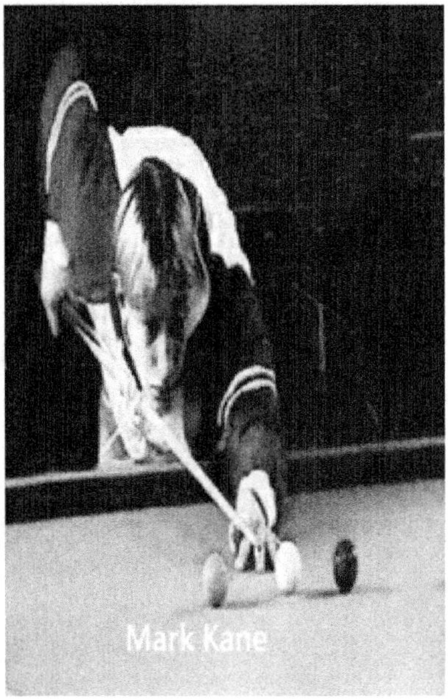

Mark Kane

Places

Easthouses Entrance to Roan's Dyke path

Newbattle entrances to Roan's Dyke Path

Roan's Dyke Path

Path behind the wall

Lane to the junction of the paths (Easthouses end)

View from the V break in the wall across the field to Reed Drive

Newbattle Road

Newbattle Abbey Crescent – Luke's street

V break

Where Jodi was found

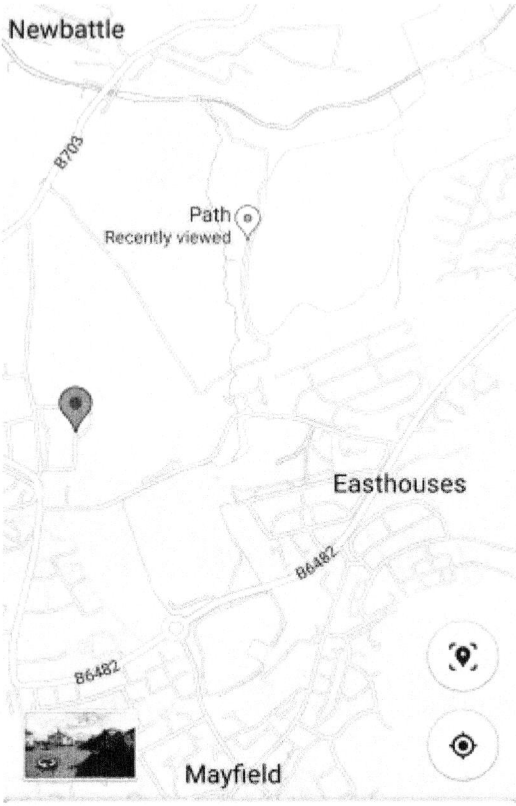

Map 1

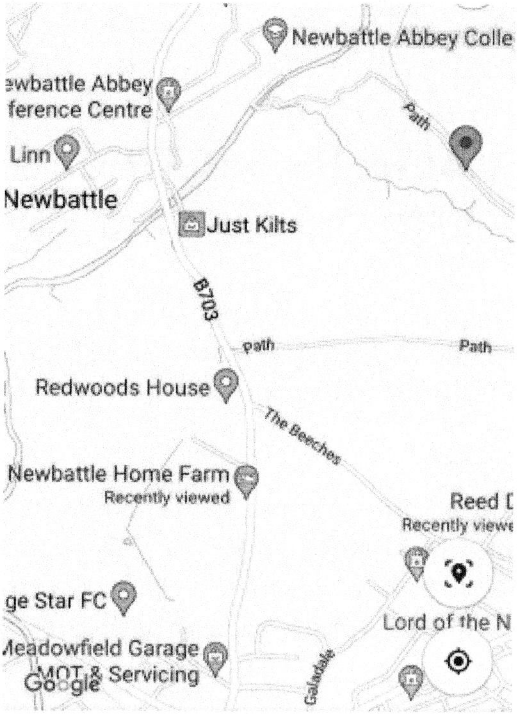
Newbattle Abbey Colle
ewbattle Abbey
ference Centre
Path
Linn
Newbattle
Just Kilts
B703
path
Path
Redwoods House
The Beeches
Newbattle Home Farm
Recently viewed
Reed [
Recently viewe
ge Star FC
Lord of the N
Meadowfield Garage
MOT & Servicing
Google
Galadale

Map 2

POACHERS, PROTECTED SITES AND BLEACH

In 2010, we looked for a `fresh pair of eyes`, as the police had done with David Dickie and later with the FBI, to understand the local area, people, and culture better.

Unlike the police, we didn't approach potential suspects *{Dalkeith CID and the relationship with David Dickie is seriously concerning and should be examined} or* anyone providing an alibi for a suspect. We also didn't ignore the advice we were given from experts.

Initially, we approached `terrier men` from Woodburn, a neighbouring estate, and `lurcher men' from the Mayfield area where Alice Walker, Stephen Kelly, Janine Jones resided and had walked from that fateful evening to search for Jodi. We also spoke with a gamekeeper from Danderhall and asked them all to show us how they would travel to the Roan's Dyke Path at Easthouses and the locus.

These men were hunters/poachers of rabbit, fox, and deer. They were men who knew the woods and surrounding areas like the backs of their hands. Between them they had over one hundred years' experience in hunting and poaching in and around the area where Jodi Jones was found.

From Woodburn at New Mills Road, we walked down a well-trodden trail, into a swing park, along a path, over a small bridge, up a small hill on worn paths, and we were in the woods at Easthouses, Jodi & Joseph's home on our left, and then we were at the junction of Lady Path and Roan's Dyke Path, where Luke Mitchell was met by the rest of the search party on the night of the 30th of June 2003 to search for Jodi, and where the jury were taken to view the break in the wall.

We travelled down Roan's Dyke Path and over the V in the wall, as it was alleged Jodi Jones and Luke Mitchell had done. We travelled on that route at my request.

We left the locus through the adjacent field and walked directly back-to-back to the junction of Lady Path and Roan's Dyke Path and onto Easthouses Road. As we walked, we witnessed others from Easthouses walking their dogs in the same field. The implication that you had to travel down Roan's Dyke Path to get to the locus, if you were coming from Easthouses, is absolute nonsense.

From Mayfield we travelled along the paths that Alice Walker, Stephen Kelly, and Janine Jones had walked the night they went in search of Jodi. We walked through the complex and onto Lady Path, and when we stopped at the junction with Roan's Dyke, I asked them to take me to the locus.

They automatically went through the large break in the wall, exactly what the local, James Falconer, had done when he went for a `clean wank` on the night Jodi was murdered. They walked into the woodland strip, past the JJ and LM engravings, and directly to the locus. They had taken a very similar route to what David Dickie had used on his way home from the locus on the 30th of June 20003.

There was no climbing walls, fences or climbing up through V in the wall and having to be assisted or persuaded. From the locus you can walk directly to Newbattle Abbey College, to Newbattle Road, to Easthouses, to Dalkeith, without ever using Roan's Dyke Path. You can walk to Reed Drive, Newtongrange, and Mayfield from the locus, only crossing over the narrow Roan's Dyke Path.

The V in the wall, and the suggestion that Jodi Jones had gone through it was, and is, nothing more than speculation at best. The importance of the V, in my opinion, was that a moped was parked there at the alleged time Jodi was murdered, and behind it, was a `gang hut`, used by the locals, including Ferris, Joseph Jones, Dickie and Mark Kane to meet up to drink and smoke hash.

The `terrier men`, poachers/hunters, were all haters of Luke Mitchell. To them he was a *"horrible beast"* who deserved to be put down, and they would have been more than willing to do it in a very cruel manner. They based their opinion on local gossip, and what they had *"read in the papers".* These men, who lay in wait for animals in the woods at night, killing them, gutting them, skinning them, who knew the area very well, and evaded the police and gamekeepers night after night in the same fields and woods, and who, after visiting the locus with me and hearing details of the time scale, the injuries to Jodi, the story of the V and Roan's Dyke Path, and that there was no DNA or blood on the alleged killer; informed me: *"it's impossible", "he couldn't have done that", "no fucking chance", "tell me the time again?"*

So, I did. I told them Luke Mitchell was allegedly seen by Andrina Bryson, at approximately 4:55 p.m. We now know that sighting is questionable to say the least, but for argument's sake, we accept it for now. Luke Mitchell then has to walk down Roan's Dyke Path, arguing with his girlfriend, coercing her over the V in the wall, fighting and struggling with her, murdering her in a brutal way, stripping her naked, tying her hand/arm, mutilating her body, escaping from the locus, going home to change his clothes, making sure there was no trace of blood or DNA, and be positivity identified on Newbattle Road at approximately 5:45 p.m. – 50 minutes later. Bear in mind the jury took 30 minutes to walk down Roan's Dyke Path and arrive at the locus.

The men told me, *"Fuck off, that's impossible".* At first the men thought I was exaggerating or lying about the times as they couldn't believe what they were hearing. The only way that was possible according to the men, *"aye nae bother, was he practised in astral projection"?* They were shocked that anyone had believed what had been explained to them.... sadly, the jury did believe it.

Later, having exhausted all of the "official" routes of enquiry, I began to consider whether the other local "sub cultures" might hold more realistic or plausible explanations. I returned to the dog men, the poachers, hunters and gamekeepers, but with a new set of questions.

Within these local communities there was a culture, or subculture, of poaching, hunting, killing and cruelty of animals, badger baiting, lamping foxes, deer, rabbits, hunting with ferrets and dogs, and snaring rabbits, foxes, and deer. Within this culture there are men who become *"addicted to killing".*

The levels of depravity and cruelty in this culture can be shocking. To give an idea of the depravity and how some in the culture and local areas view life and death, during the miner's strike in 1984, a miner from Mayfield, while on a picket line, gutted and skinned a rabbit with his bare hands, smearing the entrails onto the windscreen of a police van. This was done to shock and torment police and ended with some officers being sick. Within the local area where Jodi was murdered there are a lot of hard men, some with really brutal, cruel, and sadistic ways.

A poacher can be a person who goes out at night and gets a deer by shooting it, butchering it, carrying the kill home, and everyone in the pub, including the dogs, eats venison until its finished. It's called *"one for the pot"*.

Then there is the other poacher who shoots the deer to injure it and then sets the dogs onto the injured deer, allowing them to rip it apart. Men lie in wait in fields for foxes or deer, shooting them once the lamp startles them, or setting dogs onto them. Others just kill for the sake of killing, mutilating the animals that they kill. Wildlife crime officers could confirm that easily enough.

You could be forgiven for thinking the crime scene in the Jodi Jones murder was a poachers' kill. Alice Walker, said on finding Jodi, that it reminded her of an animal on a butcher's slab. I had to agree, sadly. The way Jodi's hand and arm was tied reminded me of a trussed carcass ready to be hung on a hook to be butchered.

The crime scene management and the questions asked of the pathologist in this case left many unanswered questions rather than answers. Dr Sandra Lean has highlighted question after question regarding forensics in this case as the pathologist's report and forensic examinations were so inconclusive in so many areas.

Professor Busuttil, however, was sure of one thing, Jodi Jones would have lost at least six litres of blood, but there was NO `blood spill` under her body or at the immediate locus, no photographs of the blood-soaked ground, the blood spray that was the locus was not *"arterial spray"* and did not reflect that of the blood lost. There were no soil reports or samples taken.

There is NO trace of the six litres of blood. There are a few drops of blood on branches lying on the floor and the `spray` on the wall is approximately four meters away from where Jodi was found lying, approximately 500 mm off the ground is a` spray` approximately 800 mm wide with the largest area of "spray" being 40 mm x 300 mm, along with some smaller spots of blood. Considering the injuries to Jodi Jones, pre and post death, the scene should have been covered in blood. Many professional people believe that Jodi was not murdered where she was found, as a result of the lack of blood.

The cadaver dogs, brought in from Yorkshire to trace the blood/death, could have answered some of these questions if they had not been hampered in their exercise by someone with knowledge of DNA and the damage bleach does to it by `cleaning` the police protected crime scene with such a substance.

Could the local subculture I'd approached offer any explanations? Professor Busutill did think the mutilations to Jodi neck could had been inflicted from the back, but there was no proof of that, and the small blood splatter appears to contradict that theory as the wall would have been covered with the arterial spray of blood. However, cutting the neck from behind fit in with the police `theory` that the killer could have killed Jodi without being covered in blood. But this didn't explain why the blood spray on the wall was so small, or why there wasn't a large pool of blood at the wall where Jodi was found. Professor Busutill did admit later, while on the BBC, that it would be *"highly unlikely"* that the killer of Jodi could inflict such injuries and not be covered in blood.

What kind of weapon was used to murder and mutilate Jodi Jones was never established. The defence wounds sustained by Jodi are similar to injuries I've witnessed on machete attack victims. Wounds inflicted by large heavy blade weapons. Dr Sandra Lean, in a consultation with a weapons expert, was informed the wounds would have been inflicted by an axe type weapon, a heavy blade, machete, bowie hunting knife or something similar.

This was never investigated, as it would have dismissed the theory about Luke Mitchell's pocketknife being missing and therefore, possibly the murder weapon. This is one of the most ludicrous suggestions I have witnessed in this case, and there are many.

These questions have always puzzled people who studied the case files. The evidence or lack of it, gave ex detectives, investigative journalists, pathologists, criminologists and hunters/poachers serious concerns and doubts that Jodi Jones had been murdered where she was found. In fact, they weren't concerns; they didn't believe Jodi was murdered where she was found, and the evidence supports that theory.

Had Jodi been murdered somewhere else and dragged or carried to where she was found is a question and concern commonly raised in this case. Scientific evidence establishes that Jodi was dragged at some point, both her hands and her feet show they had heavy contact with the soiled floor. The dirt on her hands and nails are consistent with her hands scraping the ground. Her feet were similar, and her blue ankle socks came off while being dragged only to be put back on her feet, inside out, with soil stains now on the inside of the socks.

But, in addition to there being no blood at the scene where

Jodi was found, there is no evidence of her being dragged there either. No drag marks along the soft, leaf-covered ground.

For years, scientists, lawyers, and police couldn't answer the questions raised, however for the first time in this case, having approached these "alternative experts" who were never consulted at the time, I had reasonable, believable, and plausible answers and explanations. These were provided by hunters, poachers, and a gamekeeper who, in my opinion, were expert witnesses given their knowledge.

Jodi Jones was tied up after death, or while unconscious, in a specific way. It was not with her hands tied behind her back as widely reported. One of her hands was on her stomach, with the elbow protruding out from her body at right angles, and the other hand/arm on her back, tied with legs of her trousers, taking control.

The knot on the arm with the hand on the stomach appears to have come loose, suggesting Jodi was dragged or carried by the arm, thereby loosening the knot. This would explain why one of the arms left the back and fell under the body as Jodi was released and fell to the floor.

This theory is a common one between people who know the case. More importantly the theory is supported by science. There are two blood runs on Jodi's body which defy gravity. This was never investigated or examined. The blood from both wounds run toward the head, implying that Jodi was at some point upside down, which would be consistent with being carried over a shoulder or being dropped head and shoulders first after being carried.

Poachers and gamekeepers, upon hearing the questions and

circumstances, said it sounded like a someone with knowledge and experience in poaching and hunting had killed Jodi and then created a false scent trail, thereby setting up a decoy to avoid detection - a common action by poachers.

After the kill, poachers clean the carcass of anything that would get in the way of butchery, such as branches or, in this case, Jodi's clothes. The first thing they do is tie the carcass as a way of controlling and handling it, to drag, lift, hang, butcher, and skin. For non-detection from police and gamekeepers they do not leave a blood pool, but instead separate the kill and the blood as early as possible.

They achieve this by putting a bucket under the kill to catch all the blood and entrails and dump them where they are not visible. I was told, *"Always separate the kill and the blood spill for non-detection of poaching. Put as much distance as possible between the blood spill and the carcass"*

If poachers/hunters don't have a bucket or other means to catch and dispose the blood, they bleed the animal, stabbing it in the main artery, pushing in a hosepipe, *{piping it}* and directing the blood into a stream, a tree root, soft ground, or just spread it as far and as wide as possible, separating it from the body.

If they don't have a hose pipe, they will bleed the dead body in a place that's not visible to the naked eye {long grass etc}, and then take and hide the body somewhere else. Why? To avoid detection and confuse authorities.

Could this explain the lack of blood where Jodi was found?

If Jodi Jones' body was separated and `hidden` away from the blood spill, no one cared to look for or ask where the six litres of blood had gone. The body was also hidden away from sight of the ` gang hut ` , albeit in a close location, nineteen meters away.

Moreover, Jodi's clothes, and in particular her training shoes and bra, looked like they had been purposely placed where they were found. The bra was perfectly folded and didn't have a drop of blood on it. The training shoes laces had been purposely loosened with no dirt or blood on the white laces. It's difficult to ignore the clear elements of "staging" the scene, in order for the discovery of the body to be perceived in a very specific way – i.e. that Jodi was killed, stripped and bound where she was found.

Professor Busuttil, or anyone else for that matter, could never, or was never asked, to ascertain whether the killer or killers were right or left-handed. They couldn't tell if the injuries on Jodi's body were inflicted by backhand or forehand slashing, or indeed the way the blade had been handled.

But there are two further aspects to the poacher's approach that tie, with astonishing accuracy, into other, known pieces of evidence.

Firstly, there is a possibility, supported by science, that Jodi was carried to where she was found, after she was murdered. The livor mortis on her legs establishes that soon after death *(30/40 minutes)* there was something approximately 100 mm wide putting pressure on her calf muscles which obstructed the settling of livor mortis. There is also the failure of livor mortis settling on Jodi's back around the shoulder area. This could be consistent with Jodi being carried in an "over the shoulder" position, the arm restraining her legs restricting livor mortis across the calves, and the upper half of her body, being upside down, accounting for the blood runs in the "wrong" direction mentioned earlier. This is a theory which should have been examined and investigated but, like everything else in the case, was ignored.

Secondly, there is the remaining part of the false scent trail (the first being the separation of the blood and the body) and that is bleaching, or using ammonia. For example, if a poacher had bled a deer and buried the blood and entrails, or a fighting dog was buried, it's common to spread ammonia around the spot of the burial to create a protected site, as dogs won't go past the ammonia.

When dogs from Yorkshire were requested to come to Dalkeith, who could have discovered the place of death, the locus was contaminated by a bleach like substance which prevented the dogs from doing their work. Someone had created a `protective site` using ammonia, while the police had control of the site. In particular, this would have the effect of completely concealing, from the dogs at least, the actual place where the murder took place, leaving the false impression that the place where Jodi was found was the place where she was killed.

If it wasn't the police who had done this, then it was someone with `special knowledge` of where Jodi was found. That could only be the killer, killers or someone who had moved Jodi after her death. Whoever it was had knowledge of ammonia and the effect it had on dogs, and how to protect a site they didn't want discovered by gamekeepers or police.

At the murder scene, on the day of the murder of Jodi Jones, we know that John Ferris and Gordon Dickie confessed to being there at 5:15 p.m., the very time Jodi was being murdered and mutilated.

Both these men have knowledge and lived experience in hunting, poaching, cruelty to animals, as well as avoiding detection from police and gamekeepers. The actions of separating the blood spill and the kill, burning clothes, destroying vehicles, and laying false scents trails are second nature to these men.

David Dickie has been involved in poaching and hunting for more than 40 years and we know he examined the murder scene soon after his son returned to Reed Drive after leaving the locus.

Someone or something restricted the livor mortis settling on Jodi's calf muscles and part of her back. This had to be done within 40 minutes of Jodi dying - the very time David Dickie was at the scene.

Did David Dickie move the body of Jodi Jones to set up a false scent trail to confuse the police as he has done literally thousands of times before, with animals?

David Dickie is then, at the invitation of the police, asked to visit the locus again to tell them, despite no evidence whatsoever, how Luke Mitchell had escaped towards the tool hire place on Newbattle Road. A further false scent trail? As a result of this "visit," any evidence placing Mr Dickie there now has an "innocent explanation."

Despite Dickie's two visits to the locus, there is no record of him "educating" the police on blood pools, avoiding detection, hiding the carcass, bleeding the kill, trussing it to make it easier to manage. The sole and whole topic of conversation was Luke Mitchell.

The relationship between David Dickie and Dalkeith CID is concerning to say the least. It has tinges of the Stephen Lawrence case whereby police targeted and harassed the innocent while courting their `pal`, despite him being a potential suspect or assisting the suspect. This relationship needs to be investigated.

The `stocky man`, or Joseph Jones, can be added to the above. He was an experienced poacher/hunter and the levels of cruelty or barbarity that he was capable of, is a matter that only him and others close to him would know. But what is established, is that other lads his age who were into hunting and poaching were afraid of him. Not because of his fighting skills, but because he was *"mental", "a sick bastard", "evil", "a weirdo",* and wouldn't think about going in the woods hunting with him.

Another unanswered question which we have considered for many years, is how Jodi Jones' top half of her torso was so clean, considering her t-shirt, prior to being ripped off, was saturated in blood. You could be forgiven for thinking that Jodi had been cleaned by a sponge or a cloth. Only the two small blood runs are visible on the top half of her torso.

One plausible answer was that Jodi was left out all night and exposed to the elements and foxes or other wild animals, who would lick the blood from the corpse. There are plenty of foxes in and around the woodland strip at Roan's Dyke Path.

The foxes licking the blood from the body made sense, except the poachers believe the foxes would have torn at the flesh, where most domestic dogs wouldn't.

Livor mortis, *{settling of blood after death in gravity}*, establishes that Jodi Jones was lying face down when she died. So, if foxes or dogs had been responsible for the clean torso, they wouldn't have been able to lick the front of the torso as it lay face down. Yet when Luke Mitchell and the search party discovered Jodi Jones, she was lying on her side. Livor mortis strongly implies that Jodi's body had been moved some time after death from lying face down to being on her side.

Luke Mitchell didn't touch the body. Alice Walker cradled it, but claimed never to have moved it, and both Luke Mitchell and Alice Walker described Jodi lying on her side as the crime photos show.

If Jodi was moved after death, who could have done so? Livor mortis implies that whoever had touched the body had to have done so very soon after death, within forty minutes maximum.

We know from his statements that James Falconer was 15 meters away from where Jodi Jones lay that fateful night. We don't know if he had dogs who could have licked Jodi's torso. Mia was never over the wall on the 30th of June 2003, but David Dickie and his nine spaniels were, not long after his son and Ferris turned up at his home at Reed Drive.

CRIME SCENE MANAGEMENT AND INVESTIGATION

So bad were their actions in the investigation of Jodi Jones' murder, that the Lothian and Borders Police in Dalkeith made the "Keystone Cops", fictional, humorously incompetent police, look like Sherlock Holmes. Their behaviour in the case was well below that of a reasonable professional standard.

In my opinion, the police conduct in the case against Luke Mitchell was criminally negligent. Lothian and Borders Police, nevertheless, spun it in a fashion that would make any politician proud. Chief Constable Paddy Tomkins stated that DS Craig Dobbie and his team had carried out *"police work of the highest quality".* I will let the readers judge that for themselves and while you do, try to keep this in mind: DS Craig Dobbie said *"basics"* were essential to all good police work.

Basic crime scene management is for the "purpose to control, preserve, record and recover evidence from the scene". A massive part of that is preserving DNA evidence. Preserved evidence can help to solve cases and can exonerate the innocent or help prove guilt.

The role of the crime scene management team is to ensure that potential evidence in police investigations is *"preserved, collected, analysed and ultimately used to provide proof"*, and to help demonstrate events as they occurred. Forensic science can produce all sorts of answers in a crime investigation, including those from skin cells, hair, DNA, blood, sperm, mobile phone data – all essential in a murder inquiry as horrific as the murder of Jodi Jones.

Forensic science is a critical element of criminal investigations. Forensic scientists examine and analyse evidence from crime scenes to develop first class, objective findings in order to assist the police in capturing perpetrators of crime or to absolve an innocent person from suspicion.

A crime scene was created on 30th June 2003 and, according to Lothian and Borders Police, the murder of Jodi Jones happened at 5:15 p.m. at the locus in the woods west of the V in the Wall on Roan's Dyke Path. If Jodi was murdered at 5:15 p.m., it stands to reason her assault and struggle must have happened prior to that time.

It was argued that Jodi must have been with someone she knew who was able to coerce her over the V in the wall. So *"basics"* tell us that the V, the path, and where the body was found are all a part of the crime scene. As well, the area where the "stocky man" was seen following Jodi, where Ms Bryson said she had seen Luke Mitchell on Lady Path, Reed Drive where Ferris and Dickie travelled, and the school-grounds where the search party met police and other members of Jodi family, were all part of the crime scene.

Basic police work and common sense tells you that the search party could hold vital evidence on their person. In particular, Luke Mitchell, Stephen Kelly and Alice Walker would have as they had gone over the V in the wall. Alice Walker moved and cradled the body of Jodi Jones, after which she hugged Janine. The transfer of DNA should have been of paramount importance but instead was ignored.

All their clothes should have been removed and examined for DNA and forensics. For whatever reason, they were not. At the Newbattle High School car park, Alice Walker, Stephen Kelly, and Janine Jones were permitted to gather and share their phones with other members of the family who had congregated.

By 1:45 a.m. members of the search party, excluding Luke, were taken to Newbattle Abbey Police Station and, bizarrely, the police didn't take their clothes, but instead drove Stephen, Janine, and Alice to Judith Jones' home, while keeping Judith Jones and Alan Ovens at the station to take their statements.

The only reason ever given for this incompetence came when DS Craig Dobbie admitted that he wasn't aware who was part of the search party or who had gone over the wall. The only focus was on Luke Mitchell, as he was under the impression Luke was the one who had found the body.

Now we had the search party, except for Luke who was sitting in the police station, meeting in Judith Jones' house. This house now should have been a crime scene since the police failed to get their clothes and examine them.

More importantly, Joseph Jones now had a reasonable excuse if Jodi's blood/flesh had ever been discovered on him or in the house as Alice Walker, Stephen Kelly and Janine could have taken it in with them.

Luke Mitchell on the other hand had been correctly separated from everyone, his mobile phone taken from him and, on the instructions of DS Dobbie, at 01:00 a.m. was taken to Dalkeith Police Station where he was stripped, photographed, and forensically examined.

In my opinion, the first CID on the scene at the Newbattle School car park witnessed Luke Mitchell separated from the Jones family, petting his dog, and made up their mind that Luke Mitchell was the killer and believed the case solved. Scottish Criminal Cases Review Commission accept that Luke Mitchell was a suspect when he was taken in for the *"full works"* on the night Jodi was murdered. SCCRC recognise that Luke Mitchell was the "only suspect" by the $4^{th\ of}$ July 2003.

An hour after Jodi was discovered, a Family Liaison Officer (FLO) was appointed to the Jones family, but not to Luke Mitchell, which tells me he was being considered a suspect as early as that. If he wasn't, how can they explain the botched investigation, starting with permitting the trio from the search party to walk away with possible forensics and DNA on their clothes.

DS Craig Dobbie said he wasn't aware that Stephen Kelly and Alice Walker had been over the wall or near the body. It's unimaginable to think that two witnesses, who had been at the locus with one even cradling the body, had been allowed to go home without their person or their clothing being examined.

As an afterthought, several days later the police contacted Alice Walker, Stephen Kelly, and Janine Jones to obtain the clothing they were wearing on the night of the murder. Alice Walker couldn't remember all that she had been wearing but had, nevertheless, washed her clothes and the clothes of Stephen Kelly and Janine Jones.

On the $16^{th\ of}$ July 2003, the forensic report on Luke Mitchell came back. There was NO DNA and NO forensic evidence whatsoever to link Luke Mitchell to the crime of murdering Jodi Jones.

The report said the "residue from under his nails was dirty, his hair unwashed" which indicated Luke Mitchell had not attempted to clean himself up. This must have been a huge shock to Lothian and Borders Police.

On that same day coincidentally, police called a press conference where Jodi's aunt spoke about how Jodi liked to tease her siblings {it was the other way around}. The police also took the opportunity to highlight that Jodi was always borrowing her sister Janine's clothes despite them living more than a mile apart. At the same time as the press conference, the police were advising a potential suspect, Stephen Kelly, on how he could explain why or how his sperm was on Jodi Jones T-shirt, and that was that Jodi must have borrowed it from Janine.

In addition to the above we know that James Falconer's brothers were in the crime scene area and discovered a hoodie which had been discarded at Lady Path. This was the same area the moped boys had travelled when they left the locus at 5.15 p.m., the exact time Jodi was being murdered.

If the police had forensically examined the hoodie, they would have found the DNA of James Falconer's brother and, thereafter, would have had a match for the semen found in the condom 15 metres away from Jodi's body. There was no forensic examination of the hoodie because police believed it had been dumped on the waste ground a week earlier, and therefore irrelevant to the investigation.

But there were actually TWO dark blue hoodies discovered at the crime scene. The one that belonged to James Falconer's brother, found in the long grass at Lady Path, and one found at the locus in the `gang hut` where James Falconer's condom was found. This dark blue sweatshirt was photographed but never logged as having been forensically examined. The unidentified stocky man was seen wearing a *"dark coloured sweatshirt, possibly a hoodie"* and here was one behind the V in the wall, yet not examined.

Furthermore, we know that David Dickie had been over the V in the wall with his nine spaniels the night Jodi was murdered, after his son and John Ferris admitted having been at the locus minutes before.

Instead of treating the Dickie home on Reed Drive as a crime scene by searching the house and examining all their clothes, they instead took David Dickie back to the locus, contaminating any possible evidence they could have retrieved. The relationship between Dalkeith CID and David Dickie is something that should be a matter of concern.

The police, consciously or unconsciously, did exactly what Wayne Couzens {*MET Police Officer who murdered Sarah Everard*} had done to contaminate the crime scene.

After the murder of Sarah Everard, Couzens revisited the very site where he had burned the body and played with his wife and children. He then had a reasonable explanation for his DNA being there. Lothian and Borders Police did exactly the same thing for David and Gordon Dickie.

DS Craig Dobbie said he *"wanted to eliminate all of the family members and associates of Jodi Jones and all the males who used Roan's Dyke Path".* He didn't do very well with this either. Ferris, Dickie, the `stocky man`, Falconer, Mark Kane, and Robert Greens were all missed or ignored.

At Newbattle Abbey College, located several hundred meters

away from the murder site, there were several other males living there after the term had finished and were never questioned. Robert Hall, Greens, and Mark Kane were all very familiar with the woods. They were part of an occult group who met there to drink and speak of the `other world`. In addition, Alan Knox from Jodi's village of Easthouses walked Roan's Dyke Path daily. None were questioned or ruled out.

The specific physical location where Jodi was found should have been a great provider of evidence. Instead, the police contaminated and spoiled it and, as a result, instead of producing evidence and answers, it provided nothing apart from questions and speculation. This is extraordinary, considering the nature of the murder.

There is generally an accepted theory, based on the lack of physical evidence, that Jodi Jones was not murdered where she was found, however there was no search or investigation into this possibility.

DS Craig Dobbie arrived at the crime scene at 01.00 a.m. and instructed that Luke Mitchell was to get the "full works" - stripped, photographed, and forensically examined. He ordered a team of four officers, a crime scene manager, pathologist, and photographer to film the locus. The first thing they did was to start cutting away over-hanging branches of trees to make it easier to film, immediately compromising the crime scene

Two of the identification officers gathered up Jodi's clothes before forensic officers arrived. There is no record on how these clothes were collected and packed so they weren't forensically protected. Similarly, Jodi Jones' body was rolled onto a polyethylene sheet before forensic officers arrived, even though DS Dobbie gave orders to secure the crime scene.

It is a sad fact that despite twelve experienced police officers, including DS Dobbie, being in attendance at the locus between 1 a.m. and 8 a.m., Jodi's body lay uncovered in the rain that entire time.

DS Dobbie must have known that a body should have had a canopy over it to protect it from the elements and foxes, but no cover was applied. DS Dobbie took *"full, on call responsibility"* for this mess.

Police Officer Monteith, who was left to guard the locus, said the first forensic officers arrived at 4:45 a.m., nearly 5 hours after Jodi was discovered. By that time the crime scene had been contaminated and generally ruined by the police.

The first pathologist, part of the forensic team, couldn't get over the V in the wall so just went home. She easily could have walked to either end of the path and entered the locus from there. Which was the same way James Falconer got there to have a `clean wank` and where David Dickie exited after visiting the locus soon after his boy and another had left. This left Jodi Jones out in the open and exposed to foxes and elements, rain included, for another three hours and more.

There was never an attempt to establish time of death, there are no records of body temperature, signs of rigor mortis or livor mortis, all of which could have helped establish the time of the murder and which could have eliminated certain people from the investigation.

Jodi Jones could have been murdered at any time after she left her home at around 5 p.m. according to what the police accepted from their "expert witness", Dave Dickie. He said he was at the locus at approximately 6 p.m. with his nine spaniels and didn't see the body of Jodi. James Falconer was there at *"grey dark time"* and claimed not to have seen Jodi. The question arises, if you accept the accounts of Dickie and Falconer, was Jodi at the locus at the times the men were there, or was she murdered elsewhere and taken there after Falconer had left? None of these questions were ever explored because they didn't fit in or benefit the police narrative.

Just when you thought the investigation couldn't get any worse, more astonishing incompetency transpires. Dalkeith Police, at the locus, photograph branches with spots of blood on them, then move them by hand and place them against the wall in order to put large steel plates on the path so not to trample over the ground. They then bag the branches with notes, Branch 1, Branch 2. These branches had blood spots and could have provided more forensics, however the police had contaminated them as evidence.

The steel plates ended approximately four meters from where Jodi lay. Before the forensic team arrive, crime scene photographs confirm that Dalkeith Police had either rolled Jodi onto a sheet of polyethylene and dragged her and the plastic sheet over the ground where she lay with the steel plates under her, or they dragged Jodi's body over the ground for four metres and dumped her on the polyethylene.

Forensic officer Derek Scrimger, who arrived at the locus at 8 a.m., was very kind to his colleagues when he said the scene had not been *"ideally managed".* The police had cut away branches and ivy to get better photographs, and they had trampled all over the crime scene, dragging the body of Jodi over the ground to where she lay.

On 1st July 2003, less than 10 hours after Jodi had been

discovered, the crime scene *{locus, clothes, witnesses, houses}* had been contaminated or destroyed by Dalkeith police. The only person or part of the crime scene that was uncontaminated or not destroyed was Luke Mitchell.

On the 12$^{th\ of}$ July 2003 a purse was discovered under a large boulder directly at the foot of the V in the wall. Neither the cards nor purse had been reported as missing. It must have been there for 12 days while the police "combed the scene". There were no records in the defence files as to who owned that purse.

Bin collections in the local area went ahead, thousands of pupils were permitted into the car park and school grounds where the witnesses had been the night before, all while Jodi was still lying there. To cap it all off, the crime scene was cleaned with a bleach like substance just prior to cadaver dogs arriving from Yorkshire on 10th-12th July 2003.

The police had control of the locus until the 16$^{th\ of}$ July 2003. Why they cleaned the locus with bleach, hampering the cadaver dogs work, I will leave up to the reader to decide.

After finding Malacca cane at the murder scene police brought in a Botanist and, leaving aside the Malacca cane, what he reported from the scene was disturbing. Three weeks after the murder of Jodi, he reported: *"there was lots of wood lying about, covered in blood" ......* but he didn't find any wood that was not native to the woodland.

Jodi, it was claimed by DS Dobbie, was *"hit on the head with a limb from a tree"* and yet here we had a botanist reporting weeks after the murder lots of wood coated in blood lying around. At the same time on 21st July, Scotland on Sunday said Roan's Dyke Path had just reopened after *"more than 20 police officers had spent two weeks scouring the area for clues..."* They must have either overlooked the locus or didn't think blood on wood was important.

The very spot where Jodi Jones was found was controversial as being the actual site of the murder, to say the least. There was no *"pooled blood"* where she lay and the blood spots on the wall close to where she was found included only a small amount of blood spray. Genuinely, I have seen much more blood from a broken nose in a boxing spar than I witnessed at the locus where Jodi was found. Common sense tells you that shouldn't be the case. Professor Busuttil said Jodi would have lost approximately six litres of blood with the injuries she had sustained, however there was very, very little blood at the place where she was discovered.

Moreover, Jodi Jones was dragged at some point as her feet, hands and even her socks show signs of dirt markings consistent with grabbing at the dirt with her hands and being dragged with her feet scaping the dirt. However, there was no trace of any dragging or struggle at the site.

This led to the argument, or understanding, from former police officers, pathologists, criminologists, and investigative journalists that Jodi Jones was not murdered where she was found. There was no investigation to ascertain where exactly the murder took place, and no one cared to look or examine the evidence, or lack of it, that the locus provided.

e police argued that the injuries to Jodi Jones, in particular the cutting of the throat, would not have necessarily meant the killer was covered in blood, but there is no evidence of the six litres of blood Professor Busuttil estimated was lost from Jodi's body. In fact, it was never found, or even looked for.

There was no blood under her body and very little on the wall. The pathologist said he couldn't say if the killer was left or right-handed but thought the cuts to the throat had been done from behind, supporting the *"no blood-soaked killer"* theory put forth by the police.

However, some of Jodi clothes were *"extensively stained"* with blood, her T-shirt in particular. Her trousers, which were used to tie her hands/arms, appeared to be clear of blood, her bra was spotless and folded perfectly at the locus. Her training shoes, apart from a very small bit of blood were spotless, and the laces appeared to have been loosened perfectly. Her socks were carefully put back on her feet after being off at some stage of the attack.

Jodi Jones had cuts to her face and lip, a deep slash to the arm which Professor Busuttil said would have drained her of energy and blood as it was so deep. All these injuries were committed while Jodi was alive, and it is inconceivable that the attacker or attackers didn't have blood on them. To suggest such a murder could happen without any forensic links to the killer is impossible, in my opinion, but given the police work in this case anything was possible.

There was a claim that there were teeth marks on Jodi's hand, which was rejected by the Crown, and there was no defence investigation as Legal Aid had been denied.

There were reports that there was no DNA under Jodi's fingernails, yet the report only referred to one hand and not both. It was claimed that Corinne Mitchell was asked to fund the defence investigation into DNA analysis but that she refused. Mrs Mitchell denied ever being asked and said she would have happily paid. The Legal Aid Board lost the file so it is impossible to establish why such reports were never completed.

The incompetence continued to go from bad to worse. A German army shirt which was taken from Luke Mitchell's home suddenly became a *"long parka style jacket"* and whatever your thoughts are on whether Luke Mitchell owned a parka or not, the suggestion that it was burnt in such a small burner in garden without a trace is ridiculous. Nevertheless, DS Dobbie said detectives had *"cause for suspicion concerning the wood burning stove in the Mitchell's garden".*

From the outset to anyone with a shred of common sense, the "moped boys" must have been persons of interest at the very least. They had been witnessed in and around Roan's Dyke Path and their moped seen at the locus at the very time of the murder of Jodi. We have come to accept, perhaps wrongly, that the two men on the moped were John Ferris and Gordon Dickie. This was never proven or investigated despite both Ferris and Dickie giving contradicting statements about what they were wearing on that day while on the moped. They lied to the police about their whereabouts and couldn't remember who they had seen or where they were as their moped was parked at the V in the wall.

There is a reasonable argument that one of the men could have been Joseph Jones on the moped that day with either Ferris or Dickie. He had been with Ferris all day and had planned to meet up with him again at 6 p.m. He was close to Dickie and was with him in the days prior to the murder, as well as being part owner and user of the moped.

When police asked Judith Jones months later if Joseph had a bike, she told them he had *"gotten rid of it"* - the very thing that happened to the moped. Moreover, Joseph Jones did NOT have an alibi for his whereabouts at the time of the murder.

Another reason it may have been Joseph on that moped at 5:15 p.m. on the 30th of June 2003 is that witnesses said one youth was wearing a baseball cap, the other had short dark hair. Dickie had short hair but claimed he was wearing baseball cap, contradicting Ferris who had curly hair but also claimed to be wearing a baseball cap.

If Dickie was wearing the baseball cap, who was the youth with short brown hair.... Joseph Jones? Police now had two men on a moped and both claimed to be at the very spot where Jodi was murdered, but neither could remember where they went or what they did after they dismounted from the moped at the V in the wall. This nonsense was just accepted by the police.

John Ferris went on to cut his own hair because he said he didn't want to be mistaken for the "stocky man" or *"wrongly accused` of the murder"*. The problem with this statement by Ferris is that the "stocky man" wasn't known to the police, or anyone else, when John Ferris made it.

Both men, one related and each known to Jodi Jones, had a history of serious violence towards women, lying, and drug dealing, and are at a murder scene at the time a girl was brutally murdered. They claimed they didn't know where they went or what they were doing while their moped was parked at the locus, failed to come forward to assist police or help clear themselves, and the police just accepted their story with no investigation……nothing!

John Ferris had been in and out of Jodi's house on the day of the murder and had arrangements to meet Joe Jones at 6 p.m., a meeting that was cancelled for no apparent reason and which was never investigated. Ferris said he was never out of Jodi's house with Joseph and painted a picture of them being very close friends and associates. However, after he was brought to police attention, Judith Jones tried very hard to distance herself and her family from John Ferris.

John Ferris lived with his and Jodi's granny, Alice Walker. On the 30th of June 2003, after being at the murder scene around 5:15 p.m., he went to Gordon Dickie's home and left promptly at 9 p.m. to return home because his granny *"went to bed early".* However, instead of going home he went to Yvonne Walker's flat, who was his half-sister and rumoured partner. The many accusations of incest used to smear the Mitchell family was, to me, classic projection. Everything other families in the community were guilty of were projected onto the Mitchells. John was a frequent visitor to Yvonne's flat, which was also a regular hang out for Ferris, Joe Jones, Dickie, Luke, and many others to drink, smoke, etc.

Jodi Jones was also a frequent visitor to Yvonne Walker's flat and at times stayed well past her curfew. Judith Jones claimed she called the flat on the evening of the 30th of June to ask if Jodi was there and didn't, at first, believe Yvonne Walker who claimed she wasn't. It was claimed that Ferris had to confirm to Judith that Jodi wasn't there. If this was true, John Ferris knew Judith had concerns for Jodi, yet he later saw his granny, Stephen Kelly and Janine Jones leaving from Alice Walker's house at approximately 11 p.m. and he *"didn't think anything of it".* And once again, this was all just accepted by the police.

A friend of Yvonne Walker's highlighted a pair of leather padded gloves stuffed behind a radiator in Yvonne Walker's flat, where Ferris, Joseph Jones and Dickie had been. The gloves were damp, muddy, with *"strands of brown hair"* attached. Ferris accepted that these gloves were his and he had borrowed them from his brother without him knowing and put them in a drawer with his knife. He claimed he had no idea how they had been *"submerged in water and were now stuffed behind a radiator in Yvonne Walker's flat".*

Gordon Dickie, however, claimed they were *his* gloves and he had lent them to Ferris. On the 26th of November Dickie said, *"The only other thing I remember about gloves is that sometime after the murder, John Ferris said something about his sister Yvonne finding a pair of wet gloves and giving them to police. He {Ferris} said, "I don't know if they are mine or yours, but it's a bit dodgy" ......I don't know what he meant by that but wasn't really bothered about it".*

The gloves, I'm led to believe, were the ones used by all boys using the moped. The moped had been altered, the exhaust had been cut, manifold removed, and you could hear the moped before you ever saw it. The boys frequently changed drivers and the vibrations from the moped hurt their hands, so gloves were used. But why the confusion/lies about gloves that were used by people driving a moped?

My investigations told me that Ferris was seen acting suspiciously at approximately 10 p.m. on the night Jodi Jones was killed, not far from where the gloves were found and was wearing similar gloves. This was before Jodi was even considered missing.

Despite Dickie and Ferris talking about the gloves and how finding them *"looked dodgy"*, neither Ferris nor Dickie thought to inform police about them. It was only after a female visitor to Yvonne Walker's flat found the gloves and handed them in, did Ferris and Dickie remember the gloves.

Interestingly, there is no report of forensic results from these gloves, despite them belonging to and being used by boys that were at the murder scene and had been found under suspicious circumstances.

Judith Jones, despite Ferris being close to Joseph and being at the Jones' house daily, started to attack Ferris as soon as he came forward to say he had been at the V in the wall on the 30th of June 2003, and that Alice Walker had told him not to come forward to the police.

The attacks intensified and by 24th September 2003 Judith Jones stated that she *"knew that John Ferris had spoken to police on Thursday, July 3rd* {date wrong by Judith} *after an appeal was put out for two boys on a motorbike....*she *"knew he originally said he had been on the path sometime before quarter to five", "that her gut feeling was that his original version was concocted and rehearsed so that he would remember it" ..."He was too precise...how would he remember every single detail exactly?"....* In her mind *"it sounded like it had all been worked out by the two of them {Ferris and Dickie} and* the only reason Judith could think of why Ferris and Dickie would make up such statements was *"they want absolutely nothing to do with it all".*

What did Judith Jones think Ferris and Dickie knew that they were hiding? What did they want nothing to do with? Who were they protecting? Who or what did they see at the locus at 5:15 p.m.? None of these questions were ever investigated.

Later Judith Jones claimed Ferris and Dickie were *"selfish"* and *"knew more than they were letting on"* and that they had lied to the police for selfish reasons......I concur.

But what lies and what else did they know? One thing I am sure of, if Ferris or Dickie had witnessed Luke Mitchell at the V in the wall at 5:15 p.m. when they were there, they would have had no hesitation in providing the police with that information.

By the time Luke Mitchell went to trial in January 2005, Ferris had been chased out of Dalkeith with the threat of violence from Joseph Jones and moved over sixty miles from his home. He claimed that his granny, Alice Walker, had told him that Joseph was going to *"batter him"* and, in a statement by Judith Jones, she said Joseph was going to *"have a word"* with Ferris. Why was Joseph Jones not charged with intimidating witnesses in a murder trial?

I have no fear of any reproach, when I say Joseph Jones is the `*stocky man*` who was seen following Jodi Jones on the 30th of June 2003. He was not in his mother's house all day and all night. Alice Walker was in the house and there was no report of Joseph Jones being there. Alan Ovens claimed it was Janine Jones in the house and not Joseph when he returned from work. Police were in the house after Jodi was reported missing and didn't see or hear Joseph. He wasn't seen by anyone until approximately 1 a.m. on the 1st of July 2003 at the school car park.

Judith Jones lied, and for whatever reasons, continuously lied for her son Joseph Jones. We know from records that Judith called the mental health team at 3.23 p.m. to cancel the psychiatrist's home visit on the 30th of June 2003 with the *"usual"* lies.

Joseph Jones required house visits as he was too paranoid to leave the house. Although on the day of Jodi's murder, and days prior to it, he had allegedly had a massive "breakthrough" leaving the house, walking and possibly riding a moped with Ferris and others.

Judith Jones lied for Joseph to cover up for him smoking hash, which brought on his psychosis and led to violent outbursts. Judith Jones either lied or was sadly mistaken when she was the only person to verify the whereabouts of Joseph Jones on the day of Jodi's murder.

In the days after Jodi was murdered both Ferris and Joseph

Jones were conspicuous by their absence with regard to police statements. Joseph Jones gave a short statement to police on the morning of the 1st of July 2003 to confirm his name, address and who he was in relation to Jodi Jones. He then just disappears from the investigation. There is no mention of him from Judith Jones or Alice Walker in police statements. He pops up five days later.

I have no knowledge of the mental health history of John Ferris, but records show Joseph Jones had been sectioned twice under the Mental Health Act prior to Jodi being murdered. We know through records that he was excused from giving evidence in the trial against Luke Mitchell after he had been sectioned twice, each prior to two different dates set for the trial.

He was under mental health care for days after Jodi was murdered, as he was `*upset at the murder of his sister.* although there was no mention of him smoking bucket bongs of hash for days prior to the murder, which was known to bring on his psychosis and violent outbursts.

Violent criminals, or people with knowledge of the Mental Health Act, commonly use these methods to evade police scrutiny after they commit serious violence. They ask their mental health team for help and get sectioned under the Mental Health Act. This would have been simple for Joseph Jones considering his background and his behaviour prior to the murder of Jodi.

This also gave Joseph Jones a respite from police questioning. Even if the police had requested an interview, and there are no records to suggest they did, if any statement is gained while under the Mental Health Act, generally speaking it would be inadmissible in court.

We know Joseph Jones' psychosis is brought on by smoking cannabis resin and we know he had been smoking cannabis heavily for days prior to the murder of his sister. His mother said he was *"paranoid"*, and his behaviour was *"unpredictable"*, and he was known to have violent episodes. Days after the murder, with Joseph Jones sectioned and out of the way, Judith Jones said, *"Thank goodness they didn't find out about Joseph`s illness"*.

Nine days and seven statements later, Judith Jones, started to give much more detailed statements to the police about the movements of Joseph Jones on that fateful day. The details included the exact times Ferris arrived, what was cooked, precisely how long it took to cook, how they had to cook it a bit longer, the exact times Joseph had emerged from his room, which conveniently coincided with the times the "stocky man" was seen, a detailed description of what Joseph was wearing. All of this changed and contradicted other statements.

Judith Jones suddenly had a very detailed recollection of events of the $30^{th\ of}$ June 2003. The remarkable gain in memory came at the exactly the time the police highlighted details of the "stocky man" on the 10th of June.

The detail in these statements was remarkable under normal circumstances, but these were no normal circumstances. Judith Jones, by her own admission, was drinking large vodkas from lunch time on the $30^{th\ of}$ June 2003 to late that night which, coupled with the horrific events that unfolded, to have such a detailed memory is truly remarkable.

More astonishingly, Joseph Jones, a man who couldn't leave the house because of paranoia, suddenly, when smoking the drug which instigated paranoia and psychosis, had *"remarkable breakthroughs"* and was able to leave the house and walk long distances, both of which were "out of character developments" .... a miracle.

Judith said Joseph Jones came back and forth from his room between 4 and 6 p.m. That implies he could not have been the "stocky man". Judith then claimed to have gone to the cemetery and returned home at 7 p.m. with Joseph shouting out to her from inside his room. But Joseph claimed to be *"sleeping all night".*

He apparently thereafter fell asleep, and no one saw him until approximately 10.30 p.m. when Judith woke him to tell him Jodi was missing and he wakened shouting, *"Jodi".* Apart from Judith Jones, no one else saw Joseph Jones from approximately 1 p.m. until 1 a.m.

There are many questions arising from Judith Jones' statements of events. The times she claimed Ferris was at the house didn't coincide with Ferris's own statement. He claimed he was with Dickie at the time Judith called the Doctor to cancel the home appointment, but Judith had said Ferris was in her house with Joseph smoking hash and that was the reason she called the Doctor.

Judith alleged she woke Joseph at 10:30 p.m. to inform him Jodi was missing, and he came downstairs at that time. She didn't even know for certain that Jodi Jones was missing until almost 11:00 p.m. The first police visit to the Jones' house was at 11:20 p.m. and no-one mentioned Joseph being in the house.

So, we are to believe Joseph has purportedly just been informed that his sister is missing, and the police are being notified, yet he doesn't go downstairs to comfort or support his mother when police arrive.

He also doesn't join in when a group of family members go out searching for Jodi, leaving his granny and sister to go into the dark night instead. He doesn't rush to the school car park to comfort his family after Jodi's body was discovered. Police didn't think this to be strange or anything of interest.

There is only one person, Judith Jones, who said Joseph Jones was in her house on the evening Jodi was murdered. Alan Ovens later claimed he had made a mistake when he said it was Janine Jones in the house when he came home from work and that it was, in fact, Joseph Jones and not Janine.

Joseph claimed he had been in his room all night *"sleeping"* yet Judith claimed she knew he was there by his *"moving about.*

INVESTIGATION

At this stage in the investigation, we have a psychotic relative with a history of violence with no reliable alibi, and two men known to Jodi, one a relative, at the crime scene who were told by Alice Walker not to go forward to the police. When they eventually did come forward, they were evasive and lied to the police. We have Alice Walker failing to tell the police that John Ferris lived with her and that he hadn't come home on the 30th of June 2003.

Stephen Kelly, who had climbed through the V in the wall, told the first police on the scene, *"I take you've been at mine first"*, as they approached from Reed Drive, however, was permitted to leave the scene without being examined or his clothes being taken for forensic examination. He later said, in a police statement, *"when we (himself and Janine) take our clothes off at night, we drop them on the floor and they all land up mixed together with each other in a big bundle"*, before Alice Walker washed them all. Why – and more importantly, how – did Kelly come to make such an extraordinary statement?

On the 6th of July 2003, a week after the search, Janine and Kelly handed over the clothes they believed they were wearing on the night they searched for Jodi, telling police they had been *"washed"*. Stephen Kelly described what he was wearing on the 30th of June 2003 but handed over different clothes to the police. His clothes were listed as *"jeans, a black jumper and grey top"* and that they had all been *"washed"*.

But on the 12th of July Kelly's statement said he was wearing jeans, a black t -shirt, and he put on his green, long-sleeved FCUK t-shirt. Janine confirmed this top in a statement on the 14th of July. This top was never forensically examined.

Moreover, Kelly said that when he went over the V in the wall he could *"feel the branches catching his hat".* We now have clothes and hats missing from what was worn by the search party on the night Jodi was found and the clothes the police did have had been washed.

Stephen Kelly's is the only full DNA identification found at the murder scene in 2003 from blood/semen found on Jodi's T-shirt. In any murder case, this would have had alarm bells ringing with Kelly becoming, at the very least, a person of interest. On the contrary, police became the defence team.

Stephen Kelly's whereabouts and movements on the 30th of June 2003 are questionable. Up until the 12th of July 2003, he could not account for his whereabouts on the evening of the murder between 5-6 p.m. Then, on the 12th he claimed he and Janine had been at *"Alice Walker's all day"*, despite Alice claiming differently, saying they arrived *"later on".* He then claimed to have been at his father's house for tea, between 4.30-7:00 p.m., however didn't know if they had walked or were driven there.

There was no corroborating statement from Mr Kelly Snr at the time. However in 2014, eleven years after Jodi's murder, a document was found which claimed Janine and Kelly had gone to Kelly Snr's for tea. The detail of the meal was extraordinary to say the least. It appears the memories of those in and around this case are quite remarkable.

Alan Ovens claimed Janine Jones was in his house at 4.45 p.m. when he got in from work so Janine Jones couldn't have been at Kelly's for all of the time they claimed, 4.30-7 p.m. Alan Ovens later changed his recollection of June 30th saying it was Joseph Jones and not Janine Jones who was in their house at 4.45 p.m., approximately the time given for the "stocky man" following Jodi.

Between the 14-16th July 2003 forensic results were available to the police. Two important factors were revealed. Firstly, absolutely no DNA or forensics linked Luke Mitchell to the murder of Jodi Jones. The second was a full DNA match taken from blood/semen on Jodi's T-shirt belonging to Stephen Kelly. On the 16th of July, by a `miraculous coincidence`, Jodi's aunts were holding a press conference stating Jodi borrowed her sister's clothes without asking permission. The very reason the police told Stephen Kelly why his DNA was on Jodi's T-shirt.

At no time prior to the 16th had Janine or Kelly ever mentioned Jodi borrowing her sister's clothes. The T-shirt had been recently washed, and while the blood/sperm stain had survived, no DNA belonging to Janine had. Janine and Kelly then described different T-shirts from the one Jodi was wearing. Judith Jones said she had bought both sisters identical T-shirts, however after the police had given Kelly the *"innocent transfer"* excuse for his DNA being on Jodi, the story had developed that she had borrowed Janine's T-shirt.

Weeks later, a pile of washing was taken from Jodi's bedroom and in the pile were six black T-shirts like the one she was wearing on the day she was murdered.

At first, Kelly and Janine didn't know what Jodi had been wearing the night she was murdered and there was never any mention of Jodi borrowing clothes from her sister, who had been living with Alice Walker for over three years by this time.

PHONES

In the investigation we have a compromised crime scene, missed witnesses and suspects, failure to secure clothing and people who had been at the locus. However, phones could have given a great many answers to the questions that had been missed.

The SCCRC acknowledge that Luke Mitchell was a suspect as soon as he was taken in for the *"full works"* on the night of the 30th of June. By the 3rd of July 2003 he was the only suspect.

Given what we know now about the many other people of interest, the idea that Luke Mitchell was the only suspect by the 3rd of July is simply preposterous. It tells me that the police were not interested in investigating the murder of Jodi Jones, but merely going through the motions while making sure they *"had their man"*.

Nevertheless, on the night Jodi was murdered and Luke Mitchell was clapping his dog while the Jones' all huddled and spoke in a group, a CID officer, wrongly believing Luke had been the only one that had discovered Jodi, thought Mitchell's demeanour was all wrong, and made him a suspect.

So now a suspect in a brutal murder who had used his phone soon after such a brutal crime and possibly leaving DNA, had his phone taken from him and turned off. The phone is not forensically secured, and the police then turn the phone back on to obtain the number for Luke Mitchell's mother. Later, while in the hands of the police, call logs were deleted

Despite calls being made at 5:32 and 5:40 p.m. to the landline at

Judith Jones' house from the phone taken from Luke, there were no DNA or forensic traces to Jodi or the murder. These calls were made very soon after the brutal murder, yet no trace of blood, hair, or DNA was on the phone.

Text messages sent from Luke Mitchell's phone had been deleted and, in particular, texts sent between 4:34 and 4:38 p.m. arranging to meet Jodi. These messages were easily obtained from the phone provider who save the data for a year. There is no record of police or Luke Mitchell's defence team trying to obtain them.

Now we have Luke Mitchell's phone with no links to the murder being used to suppose his whereabouts and movements. The police argued the call to the speaking clock at 4: 54 p.m. established that he was on his way to meet Jodi. The calls to Judith Jones' landline at 5:32 & 5:40 p.m. police alleged was him constructing his alibis.

In total contrast, this *"first rate"* police investigation ignored the phones of others in the investigation. It took the police five weeks to gather phones belonging to people of interest. After the 16th of July, seventeen days after Jodi's murder, and when the forensic reports cleared Luke Mitchell, did the police take control of phones that could provide evidence. Too little, too late.

By the time the phones were collected statements had been changed, whereabouts changed, the stocky man now had an alibi, and Ferris and Dickie had changed their stories, but the phones were gathered, nevertheless.

If the crime scene management and investigation are shocking, the phone examinations are as bad. Firstly, the phones belonging to Judith, Jodi, Janine, and Joseph Jones raised serious questions and complicated matters no end.

One phone was used by Judith and Joseph but was registered to Jodi Jones. A phone used by Jodi was registered to Joseph, a phone used by Janine was registered to Judith, and of the three phones used by Joseph, one was registered to an unknown person. To complicate matters further, Janine Jones shared a phone with John Ferris and Yvonne Walker. Joseph, Janine, and Judith Jones had two numbers for John Ferris. Judith having two numbers for him was troubling as she claimed not to like him and had distanced herself from him.

KEYSTONE COPS

Police collected the phones and labelled them all incorrectly. They then claimed to have rectified the mistakes when a police officer, based solely on his memory, changed the labels to indicate who owned each phone. The remarkable memories in Dalkeith never cease to amaze. Unfortunately, the fact is no-one knew which handset belonged to who.

Then the forensics examination didn't say if the information was obtained from an actual phone handset or a transferable SIM card, despite all parties concerned admitting they frequently changed and swapped handsets.

999 logs show the call made from Stephen Kelly, which he said he made from Janine's phone, was not logged to the number attributed to Janine Jones in this investigation. If it was Stephen Kelly's phone you would think that a man with DNA links to the murder and who helped discover the body and called 999 while at the locus would have his phone taken as an important piece of evidence for examination. It was never checked by police who owned the phone that made the 999 call.

Again, mobile phones could have provided answers to many unanswered questions and assisted in solving who murdered Jodi Jones. But like every other aspect of the case, the police failed miserably. No-one knew who owned what phone or sim card and no-one knew who called whom or when......nothing.

SELECTIVE BLINDNESS

The police were very selective in which records were produced and there were very few records of calls which could have corroborated statements of some of the people of interest in this case.

Gordon Dickie had a phone, registered to his father David, which shows some activity from his phone but no records of his calls on the 30th of June 2003. A man who had lied to police about his whereabouts at the time of the murder, and who had later confessed to being at the locus at the time of the murder, didn't have his phone records checked for the date of the murder. Common sense tells you he should have.

Similarly, there are no full records of Alice Walker's mobile or land line, or records of the phones claimed to be owned by Janine Jones, Kelly, Joseph, or Ferris.

John Ferris had arranged to meet back up with Joseph Jones at 6 p.m. at Easthouses but didn't turn up. Phone records could have established the reason the meeting didn't go ahead at such a crucial time in the investigation.

There was a text message which made Ferris leave Gordon Dickie's at 9 p.m. and which was never retrieved or examined. Ferris claimed that Alice Walker called Yvonne Walker just after 10.00 p.m. looking for Jodi and Ferris had to take the phone and convince Alice that Jodi wasn't with them. (The exact circumstances in which it was earlier claimed that Judith called Yvonne Walker).

Judith and Alice denied this call. Alice could have only known about Jodi not being with Luke after 10:47 p.m., so did Ferris get the times wrong or did Alice have concerns about Jodi much earlier? Ferris claimed the 10 o'clock news was on when Alice first called Yvonne. These calls were never investigated.

Similarly, Alice Walker's land line records were very selective. Only calls up until 11.06 p.m. and only calls from Judith Jones were recorded by the police.

We know that Alice Walker called her land line from her mobile while out with the search party, but we cannot say who was left in her house on the night of the murder. If it was Joseph, this could have been easily answered by phone records.

If Joseph Jones was sleeping all night, as he claimed, phone records could establish he hadn't called, texted, or responded to incoming calls. There is no record of such investigation.

At 10:45 p.m. on the night of the murder, a female made a call to Dalkeith Police claiming to be Judith Jones and reported Jodi missing.

At 10:45 p.m. however, Judith was on the phone to Alice Walker's land line, so it wasn't Judith who made the call. But the person who did make the call knew Jodi was missing before anyone else and three minutes after Judith had asked Luke if Jodi was with him. This caller was never identified.

At 10:55 p.m. a call was recorded from Judith Jones' land line to a number attributed to Janine Jones, John Ferris, and Yvonne Walker. Another call was made at 11:18 p.m. to a number attributed solely to Janine Jones to tell her police were at Judith's house as result of Jodi being reported missing. Two calls, supposedly to Janine, but to two different numbers.

The first number called at 10:55 p.m. was a number used by John Ferris and his half-sister and partner, Yvonne Walker. Records show that there were no other call logs from Judith's phone to that number. At 10:55 p.m. Ferris and Yvonne were together. So Judith Jones was calling either John Ferris or Yvonne Walker. Why would she say it was Janine she was calling? And why would John Ferris claim he didn't know anything about Jodi when he saw his granny and others in the search party as they walked past Yvonne Walker's flat after 11:00 p.m.?

When Jodi Jones' body was discovered, Judith claimed she ran out of the house towards Roan's Dyke Path. Police statements confirm they had to hold Judith Jones back at the start of the path. Later she claimed that Joseph ran out the house toward the path, followed by herself and Alan Ovens. No one had seen or mentioned Joseph at this time.

Phone records could have also established how and why Judith's sisters had gone straight to Newbattle School car park rather than to Judith's house, a few hundred yards away, after hearing the terrible news that Jodi's body had been found. How did they know where to meet?

They were at the car park before the search party got there, despite them travelling from Bonnyrigg, 15 minutes away. Perhaps Alice Walker had called them from the murder scene and they had driven to the school car park on a hunch, but there are no records to support that.

How did Judith Jones and Joseph Jones know what wood to run to when they were informed a body had been found? From Judith Jones' home at Park Head Place, there are six woodlands, yet Joseph and Judith knew exactly which one to go to?

Records show that Alice Walker called Judith Jones at 11:53 p.m., a call that lasted 26 seconds. There is no record of what the call was about however Judith could have been informed by Alice the body was at Roan's Dyke Path. That would have provided a simple explanation as to why everyone knew to go to Roan's Dyke Path but again, none of the calls were ever investigated.

- 10:38 p.m., 8 minutes prior to a female calling police to report Jodi missing, Judith Jones texts Luke Mitchell with a message for Jodi saying she was being grounded for being out late.

- 10:40 p.m. Luke Mitchell calls Judith to tell her he hadn't seen Jodi and had no contact with her for more than 6 hours.

- 10:44 p.m. Judith Jones calls Alice Walker's land line to see if Jodi is there. {2 min call}

- (10:46 p.m. Did the search party trio head out in search of Jodi, at the very time a call was made to police reporting Jodi missing? Their later claim was that they left after the 11.03pm call from Judith)

- 10:49 p.m. Judith calls Luke to say she had *"called all of Jodi's friends" {Judith had called her mother and no other friends and had made an unanswered call to Yvonne Walker's flat}* and as Jodi wasn't with her any of her friends, she was calling police. Luke Mitchell got his dog and torch and went out looking for Jodi Jones, heading to the path that she was supposed to travel down earlier in the evening.

Records shows that Luke Mitchell had no contact with any of the trio search party that fateful night so he couldn't have told them to where he planned to walk.

The questions which puzzle me are, why did the search party go straight to Roan's Dyke Path and how did they get there so quickly?

They must have walked briskly from Mayfield without stopping or searching any other place. The trio walked past Yvonne Walker's flat with Ferris at the window. Despite Alice Walker not believing Yvonne when she said Jodi wasn't in the flat, it never occurred to her to check the flat as she walked past, but instead headed straight to Roan's Dyke Path, and then insisting on going back down the path which Luke had just travelled up.

It wasn't uncommon for Jodi Jones to be out much later than 10:49 p.m., particularly when she was at Yvonne Walker's flat. Judith didn't get a response from that flat and immediately wanted to call the police. Judith said she *"just knew"* something was wrong. Stephen Kelly said that when Judith Jones called Janine at 10:30 p.m. he *"just knew something was wrong"* .... a great deal of *"just knowing"*.

- 10:59 p.m. Judith calls Luke Mitchell just as he sets of looking for Jodi - he was at the beginning of Roan's Dyke Path.

- 11:03 p.m. Judith Jones calls Alice Walker on her land line and Alice tells Judith to call the police. Luke Mitchell had been looking for Jodi for 13 minutes by this time.

- 11:04 p.m. call from Judith to 192 to get local police station number.

- 11:06 p.m. call registered to Alice Walker's land line......no one ever investigated or discovered who was left behind in Alice Walker's that night.

- 11:18 p.m. Judith Jones called Janine on a number that had been called many times before, but different to the one she called at 10:55 p.m. Janine told her she was in the *"complex"* with Stephen Kelly and Alice Walker. It was in this call Judith told them the police were in her house.

- 11:20 p.m.- Two police officers logged their calls as being in Judith's house, for over a forty-minute period, in which Joseph Jones isn't there or mentioned. Where was he? Phone records could have established his whereabouts and who he had spoken to. No investigation was carried out.

What followed after with the police investigation was nothing short of *"selective blindness"*. With the crime scene destroyed and contaminated, witnesses missed or ignored, evidence destroyed, you would think the telephone logs and examinations would reveal the whereabouts of those involved with Jodi Jones on the day of the murder. But like the crime scene, the massive amount of evidence which could have been ascertained by phones was destroyed, wasted, not investigated or hidden from the defence team of Mitchell.

The investigation, botched or sabotaged, was so bad that even after Luke Mitchell was convicted, the public, police and media were no further forward as to why Jodi Jones was murdered.

THE BREAK IN THE WALL……THE V

There was a lot of nonsense in this case fed to the public and members of the jury through the media, including that of the break in the wall, or the "V".

DS Craig Dobbie invented a story about Luke Mitchell arguing with Jodi Jones, and as they walked down Roan's Dyke Path, went over the V in the wall. He claimed that as it wasn't an easy access, Jodi would only have gone over there with someone she knew, someone who could coerce her over the wall. Alan Turnbull, QC for the prosecution, put great emphasis on this at trial. How, or why, Luke Mitchell's defence team didn't destroy this total fabrication is beyond me.

There was that much emphasis put on the V in the wall, that on the 18th of Dec 2004, the Jury in the case were invited to take the "eeriest short country walk" under police guard and with Luke Mitchell, to witness for themselves the locus where the mutilated body of Jodi had been found. This was despite the court showing a video and photographs of the locus which was directly behind the stone wall, the V with its missing stones being the access. Lord Nimmo Smith told the Jury that the trip would *"enable you the better to understand the evidence which we have heard and are going to hear about the path and the wall and the general lie of the land".* If you didn't know better, you could be excused for believing that Lord Nimmo Smith was working for the prosecution.

On the *"locus inspection",* the jury were invited to climb through the V in the wall, helping establish that it wasn't an easy climb for small or unfit people.

The whole thing was like a stage play for the benefit of the prosecution, with Lord Nimmo Smith telling the Jury, *"You might want to decide among yourselves which places you are particularly interested in looking at" and* permitting the media to report on the locus inspection as it took place. Alan Turnbull QC had recently successfully acquired a conviction in a Scottish Court in the Netherlands of Abdelbaset al Megrahi, for the Lockerbie bombing by using props and playing to the media and jury.

In the stage-managed performance, the jury were taken through Edinburgh in convoy buses, led and escorted by police motor bikes and cars. The first stop was Easthouses, where roads were closed, and the buses slowed as they passed Jodi's house on Park Head Place. Police stood guard at Roan's Dyke Path, with the entrance covered in sunflowers and tributes to Jodi.

The Jurors stopped at the corner where Lady Path and Roan's Dyke Path meet and then headed down Roan's Dyke Path, exactly the way the police and Crown had said Luke and Jodi had gone. On the path it was highlighted how popular Roan's Dyke Path was as a short cut between Easthouses and Newbattle, which was evident by all the litter that had been dropped along the path.

The Jury, after spending time climbing through the V in the wall and examining the locus, emerged at the entrance to Roan's Dyke Path at Newbattle Road thirty minutes later. Again, there were sunflowers and tributes to Jodi at the path entrance. They left no room for doubt, by the way the locus inspection had been managed with tributes at each end of the path, that Jodi and Luke had walked down Roan's Dyke Path and that Jodi had climbed over the V in the wall. To add more drama, after the jury emerged from Roan's Dyke Path at the Newbattle entrance and were waiting on their buses, Luke Mitchell's lawyer, Ms. Law, collapses, faints or falls over, and security guards immediately pounce on Luke Mitchell, as the jury looked on.

So much importance was placed on the V and Jodi climbing through it that the day after the locus inspection, in the High Court Halls QC Turnbull had had a specially built wall, complete with the V, to sit on display inside the court Hall.

He stood Stephen Kelly, Alice Walker, and Janine Jones next to the V while he stood metres away, pretending he had a torch, and attempted to re-enact Luke Mitchell on the night the search party found Jodi Jones. His re-enactment was nothing like was described by any of the search party, as none were at the V when Luke Mitchell's dog reacted at the wall.

Nevertheless Jurors were again shown the V and how it looked with Alice Walker, Janine Jones, and Stephen Kelly standing next to it to show how difficult it was to go through, and that Jodi would have to have been persuaded or helped to go there and therefore, would had to have gone there with someone she knew.

Alice Walker claimed that with the Andrina Bryson sighting the person who helped or persuaded Jodi to go over the wall had to be Luke Mitchell. Alice must have forgotten that Dickie and Ferris, the two boys she advised not to go forward to the police, were related and knew Jodi well.

On their locus inspection, the Jury stopped at the junction of

Lady Path *(heading to Reed Drive)* and Roan's Dyke Path *(heading towards Newbattle)* where they could look back and see where Ms Bryson had claimed to have witnessed Luke Mitchell arguing with a girl, suspected to be Jodi. They could look along Lady Path towards Newtongrange and look down the path towards Newbattle, where they were shown a large break in the wall. Not a V that you had to climb over, but a break in the wall that you could walk into, taking you directly into the woodland strip where Jodi had been found.

Jurors were told that in that break in the wall, the initials LM and JJ were carved in a tree approximately 50 metres from where the Jury were standing, yet no one thought it was a good idea to enter the woods from that spot to examine the initials.

More importantly, no one thought to show the Jury you could enter the woods, and in particular the locus, from that very spot. The Jury was only aware of the V in the wall.

If James Falconer had been known to the defence and Jury, would it have made a difference? Bear in mind James Falconer was a local man, who knew the area well and who, from the very spot the Jury stood where Lady Path and Roan's Dyke meet, did NOT travel down Roan's Dyke Path, but instead went through the break in the wall and had his "clean wank" 15 metres away from where Jodi was found.

Jodi Jones, and whoever was following her that fateful night, could have taken the same path as James Falconer.

Moreover, David Dickie, on the 30th of June 2003, claimed he went over the V in the wall with his nine spaniels, after leaving his son and Ferris in the house at Reed Drive. Over the V he claimed he saw nothing of Jodi, nor did any of his dogs. He claimed to have turned right after going over the V, and simply walked up through the wooded strip and through the break in the wall, where the jury had been, before heading back to Reed Drive using Lady Path.

If the defence team had done their job and examined the local area, they would have been aware that from where the Jury stood to look down Roan's Dyke Path, it also provided a direct route to the murder scene and could, and should, have been shown to the Jury. Two local men, Dickie, and Falconer had established that fact.

In my opinion, the Jury were acting on their emotions being stirred up by the media, and emotions and reason cannot co-exist. They would have believed anything after what was told to them by the media.

THE BLACK DAHLIA

The similarities between Jodi Jones and Elizabeth Short, known as the Black Dahlia, were just that they were brutal murders of white females, both had a stab wound directly between the eyes, with horrific mutilation. Although the mutilation of Elizabeth Short was to a much greater extent.

However, if this was a factor ,Mark Kane, who was living a couple of hundred yards from Luke Mitchell, had a sick obsession with mutilated corpses. His phone and hard drive would have provided much more than just Elizabeth Short.

Moreover, if the similarities between murder victims was to be taken seriously in this investigation, then Jack the Ripper victims would have to be considered. The scarring and mutilations are similar in Jodi Jones to all the Jack the Rippers victims.

The first victim of Jack the Ripper, Mary Ann Nicholls, had injuries remarkably close to that of Jodi Jones; the scarring and mutilation of the eyes was very comparable. His last victim, Mary Ann Kelly (Nicholson), had injuries more similar to Jodi Jones than that of Elizabeth Short.

In addition to similar wounds as Jack the Ripper victims, Jodi Jones' arm was tied in a very particular fashion, at a right angle from the body in the same fashion as the Ripper's victims, which many historians argue were Freemason symbols/signs. One of Jodi's hands was on her back, the other on her stomach, in a similar position to the `*hidden hand*` which is another Freemason symbol/sign.

Given all that, is it acceptable to go around questioning and accusing Jack the Ripper `fans` in and around Dalkeith, or suspecting every Freemason who has knowledge of the Hiram Abiff and the punishment handed out to his killers. The Three Jews, Jubela, Jubelo, and Jubelum, whose mutilations in their murder were all attributed to the victims of Jack the Ripper and could easily be attributed to Jodi Jones murder, if the Elizabeth Short murder can be.

The police focused on Luke's involvement with *"goth subculture, satanism or chronic cannabis abuse"*, which was something I just couldn't buy into. I believed it to be utter nonsense.

Growing up the 1980`s we had punks who dyed their hair, had facial piercings, and spat on each other as they pogo-ed on the dance floor. That didn't make them murderers and in fact, most went onto become tree huggers or green voters.

Nevertheless, the police operation into the murder of Jodi Jones focused on the `*goth culture*` of a fourteen-year boy in the middle-class suburb of Newbattle, who bought a Music magazine with a goth rocker in it. They appeared to have overlooked the fact the murder of Jodi Jones had occurred in and around mining villages in Midlothian, Easthouses, Mayfield, Woodburn, Reed Drive, Newtongrange. Dalkeith being the local town.

Within these communities there was a culture, or subculture, as has already been discussed, of poaching, hunting, killing and cruelty of animals, badger baiting, lamping foxes, deer, rabbits, hunting with ferrets and dogs, and snaring rabbits, foxes, and deer. Within this culture there are men who become *"addicted to killing"*.

A study found that 100% of sexual homicide *{Jodi Jones murder has been described as a "lustful" murder by the FBI}* offenders examined had a history of animal cruelty. Cruelty of animals is normally a red flag in the backgrounds of rapists and murderers. According to the FBI ` s Ressler, *"these are kids who never learnt it's wrong to poke out a puppy's eyes".*

Yet Lothian and Borders Police ignored animal barbarity in Gordon Dickie, John Ferris, David Dickie, Joseph Jones, and Mark Kane and concentrated their efforts on a boy with no history of violence or cruelty towards animals, or anyone for that matter.

On the contrary, Luke Mitchell had a history of loving and caring for animals as he had been brought up to do. In 2014, when Corinne Mitchell sold the family home, trolls visited the home and then reported to the media *"his room was decorated in red, black, and grey with a big wolf on the wall" ...." the weirdest thing was the garage, which was full of clutter but also had a cage with a hedgehog in it which she had rescued. They all seemed to love animals. There were pictures of all the dogs she'd owned and a picture of Luke on a horse"*

Professor Busuttil was never asked to examine the wounds with the possibility that Jodi had been upside down, her head the closest to the ground, with the killer or killers stabbing and slashing down the way rather than up, the way they would if they had been behind her. He was the police pathologist and only provided answers to questions posed by the investigating police - answers which also fit in with their narrative.

In HMA v Sean Toal, Grant Young, Garry Orr, and David Winders, Orr and Winters were acquitted because the forensics reports were considered to be prejudiced because they had been written on police letterhead, despite the forensic team being self-employed and only working for the police in the case. Ironically,

Donald Findlay QC, was defending counsel for Orr, however no such rules or `legal victories` against Alan Turnbull QC in the Luke Mitchell case.

More ironically, Professor Busuttil, who was employed by the Crown, wrongly found that a knife with the blood of the victim and the fingerprints of Grant Young could not be the knife that killed the victim as the knife was *"too wide"*. Grant Young was cleared of the murder as a result of Professor Busuttil's findings and Sean Toal was wrongly convicted.

After years of legal wrangling with the Crown, access to the knives in the case was obtained and re-examined by Professor Pounder. He found that the knife dismissed by Professor Busuttil was indeed the murder weapon and should not been rejected. A murderer had walked free and an innocent man sent to prison because the pathology reports had been one sided. Only questions which suited the Crown's narrative were ever asked.... very similar in the case against HMA v Luke Mitchell.

When Professor Busuttil was approached with the report by Professor Pounder he, unlike most, admitted his mistake and did similarly in this case when the BBC asked him if a person or person could inflict the injuries on Jodi Jones and not be covered in blood..." *very unlikely*" he said, where before it was *"possible"*.

The questions asked by the police only fit their narrative and, as a result, the questions about poachers, blood pool, blood spray, left-handed, right-handed, all remain unanswered.

CONCLUSION

June 30th, 2022, marked the nineteenth anniversary of the murder of Jodi Jones and, sadly, there has been no closure on the case. A dark cloud still hangs over Dalkeith and the local communities, as more and more people, including people in the media, begin to question the conviction of Jodi's boyfriend, Luke Mitchell.

From the outset Luke was the one and only suspect and, without a thread of evidence and with the help of their friends in the media, Lothian and Borders Police started to create a monster out of a schoolboy, a child with no previous criminal convictions or history of violence.

Five days into the so-called investigation Luke was all over the media as the only suspect and the police were not looking for anyone else. In addition to a monster, they created a `one-horse race` with everything the police had, their reputation, salary and pensions, riding on him being the killer.

This applied to hack reporters such as Ms. Hamilton, a close pal of DS Dobbie and all but in name a police officer, who had been strategically placed within the Jones' family and was instrumental in helping frame, stitch up, and make a murderer out of a fourteen-year-old schoolboy, all without a thread of evidence.

The arrogance shown by the police was so much so that, at best, they went through the motions in their investigation as they waited on the forensic report they had requested, after stripping, photographing, taking mouth swabs, hair samples and nail scrapings from Luke, early on the morning of the 1st of July 2003, only a couple of hours after the mutilated body of Jodi had been found.

When Luke was given the "full works" he was unwashed, his ankles, wrists, hands, and hair were dirty. The residue under his nails was old. In short, he had not showered or bathed.

When the forensic report did come through on the 16th of July 2003 there was no forensic evidence that could link Luke to the murder of Jodi.... none!

Given the nature of Jodi's murder that report should have cleared Luke Mitchell, but instead the police and media hacks intensified their attacks on the boy for approximately ten months until the police charged him. By that time Luke was assumed guilty of the murder, irrespective of evidence.

Ms. Hamilton and her pals created a monster of a child and his family, again without evidence. They alleged Luke was having sexual relationships with his mother, *"he is shagging his ma,"* he was *"evil,"* he was a torturer of animals, hangings dogs from doorways. The smears didn't stop at Luke - his whole family was targeted. They said his brother, Shane, was a psychopath who had killed Jodi and Luke was taking the blame to protect their mother's first born.

Anyone who dared to speak out in defense of Luke, or to question police tactics, were targeted by the media with lies and character attacks and I have no doubt this will be the case after this book is released.

From the outset the police investigation was shambolic, to say the least. Luke was the only suspect ever considered in this case. The whole investigation was based on a hunch that Luke was the killer because he looked too calm as he sat on a pavement, clapping his dog, while Jodi's family were all huddled together talking shortly after Jodi's body had been found. This hunch led to Luke's phone being seized and he was escorted to the police station to receive the full works.

However, while Luke was being investigated the rest of the search party were driven from the police station to Jodi's house without being examined or their clothes being taken for forensic samples. The police had failed to ascertain who it was who had found Jodi. Instead, they believed it was only Luke who had been there. There was now potential forensic evidence missed as crucial witnesses were permitted to mix with others and within a potential crime scene.

The investigation and police conduct continued to get worse. The crime scene was botched and had been destroyed by Dalkeith police by the time the forensic team arrived in the morning. Jodi was left out all night open to the elements, including rain and foxes, without being covered. The police pathologist who was first to arrive was not fit enough to climb over the V in the wall and was too idle to walk into the scene from the other routes, so just went home.

The first police on the scene trampled all over the crime scene as they were cutting away branches and ivy to get better pictures. They took photographs of many branches and sticks with spots of blood on them, and then simply bagged them, destroying any potential forensic evidence. They rolled Jodi's body onto a sheet of polyethylene and dragged her from where she lay right across the crime scene, in order to get better photographs.

By the time the first of the forensic team arrived in the morning, Dalkeith Police had missed the opportunity to get evidence from witnesses who had been at the crime scene, one even touching the body of Jodi. They had failed to secure the phones of the three members of the search party.

Most importantly though was that they had irreparably damaged the crime scene where Jodi was found.

Weeks after the murder of Jodi, a botanist who was asked by police to look at the scene for Malacca cane, reported seeing blood splattered branches all over the place.

The stone which lies at the bottom of the V where people had been climbing through, had a purse underneath it which wasn't discovered for twelve days after the murder.

There were TWO dark blue sweatshirts found at the crime scene. One was found on Lady Path where the moped men had escaped in the long grass. It belonged to James Falconer's brother but dismissed as not worthy of forensic examination as it had been in the field for a week and therefore not "relevant".

The second one was found at the locus in a similar place to where Falconer's condom was found. The stocky man was reported to be wearing a dark sweatshirt. Yet no records of it are in the files or of any forensic tests ever being carried out on the sweatshirt. It was simply bagged and forgotten about. The only reason we discovered it recently was in examining the crime scene.

One dark blue hoodie is photographed in the long grass on Lady Path. This was recorded and bagged and dismissed. The other, a similar colour, was photographed at the locus, bagged, and never examined or even logged as evidence. The logical answer was that the police had overlooked it or confused it with the other sweatshirt.

Common sense tells you that such a barbaric crime, with people crawling all over it, should have provided mountains of forensic evidence. Instead, the whole crime scene, including the locus, paths, fields, people, and houses, provided NOTHING. No DNA, no fingerprints, no hair samples, no blood, nothing to connect Luke Mitchell to the crime. The failings are astonishing. The only thing that the forensics examination provided in this case was to raise more questions rather than answers.

The foremost question is, was Jodi killed where she was found?

In my opinion, and one shared by criminologists, crime scene managers, former police, forensic scientists, and other `expert witnesses` is that where Jodi was found is NOT where she was murdered.

Firstly, there is no evidence of a struggle at the accepted locus, despite the nature of the fight which took place. Jodi had mud on her feet and hands consistent with being dragged and pulled. Yet there are no signs of that in the soft ground or in the leaves.

Secondly, there is no blood spill or blood pool. I've seen more from a nosebleed than was present at the locus, and that's not an exaggeration. There are tiny spots on some branches and some larger spots on a wall approximately three metres away from where Jodi lay. There is no arterial spray and no blood spill, so where were the six litres of blood that Jodi should have lost?

No one ever cared to look, and when dogs from Yorkshire were requested to come to Dalkeith who could have discovered the place of death, the locus was contaminated by a bleach-like substance which prevented the dogs from doing their work.

Someone had created a `protective site` using ammonia, while the police had control of the site.

If it wasn't the police who had done this, then it was someone with special knowledge of where Jodi was found. That could only be the killer, killers, or someone who had moved Jodi after her death. Whoever it was had knowledge of ammonia and the effect it had on dogs, and how to protect a site they didn't want discovered by gamekeepers or police.

Thirdly, medical science, specifically livor mortis, establishes that Jodi died while she was face down. When she was found she was on her side. Livor mortis also shows that someone's arms or something similar, prevented livor mortis from forming on Jodi calf muscles and back, which could be consistent with being carried in a similar way as over the threshold, or over a shoulder and whoever moved the body would had to have been at the locus within half an hour of death.

Fourthly, there are two blood runs on Jodi body that defy gravity as they run towards the head instead of the feet. This implies that at some stage Jodi's feet had been elevated above her head. Whether that was when she was moved and dropped head and shoulders first, or done purposely to help drain her of blood before she was moved, I don't have the answer to. But it's clear she was moved and at some stage and her feet were elevated above her head.

Jodi's body was covered in `short colourless hairs` which were never examined. Over the years, Dr Lean has argued that Jodi could have possibly been wrapped in a dog blanket at some stage. Some, with no knowledge of the local area or culture, dismissed this out of hand.

However, the first `dog man` I had ever met in the local area had buried literally hundreds of greyhounds in and around the local area where Jodi was found. For an insight into the local area and how cunning some dog men can be, please watch Wallyford Dogs Odyssey 1995. An amateur vet from Easthouses, Jodi's village, is featured.

It would not be uncommon or out of the ordinary for a dog to be carried under a blanket to be buried in the woods in and around Easthouses. I'm of the opinion that instead of a dog blanket, the man or men who moved Jodi were covered in dog hairs.

The locus where Jodi was found was described to me as a poacher's kill, or a manufactured poacher's site, to draw the attention away from where she was murdered.

It was set up with Jodi's clothes being laid out in a strange fashion. Her training shoelaces had been loosened and the shoes were lying close together, facing in different directions despite coming off while being dragged along the floor. Her bra was carefully folded which, generally speaking, only women do with one bra cup inside the other and carefully placed on the ground. There was no blood on it despite the t-shirt being soaked. Her light blue ankle socks had been removed at some stage as mud consistent with being dragged was on her feet and the outside of her socks, before someone put them back on inside out.

If the failings in the forensic examination, gave no answers and only created unanswered questions, then the police investigation was no better. They failed miserably in this case.

While police targeted a fourteen-year boy on a hunch and concentrated all their efforts on him, they got their hack reporter pals to smear and destroy his family despite there being no evidence, and they failed to investigate many other possible suspects or people of interest.

Mark Kane was reported to police the day after the murder of Jodi as acting suspicions with visible scratches on his face. Kane had a history of heavy violence, torture, and cruelty towards animals and had a fascination and obsession with mutilated corpses. He was in the woods in Newbattle on the day of the murder. Several witness statements said they were concerned about him and his behaviour on the day of the murder and the days that followed.

He was in Dalkeith Police station on the 2nd of July 2003, after I took him there, in order to be eliminated as a suspect at least. Police took his details, and noted he was to *be "traced and questioned."* Despite living locally, a few hundred yards away from the police station, police never traced him or questioned him. It was after Luke was convicted when they eventually spoke to him. Then, with the help of their hack pal, they `cleared him of any involvement` as a tutor couldn't remember an essay he had written three years earlier.

I have never accused Mark Kane of murdering Jodi. Others and I rightly had suspicions about the possibility that he could have been involved. Some of his closest pals were suspicious. They reported that after the murder, *"it was like he was trying to make us believe he had done it."* His unhealthy obsession with mutilated corpses increased to sex with mutilated corpses after the murder. Anyone who reads the case files or investigates the case, including former police, criminologists, and psychologists all agree Mark Kane was, at the very least, a person of interest who should have been questioned .... but he wasn't.

Joseph Jones is, without a doubt, a serious suspect in the murder of his sister. He was violent, psychotic, paranoid, known for his violent outbursts, and had been sectioned under the Mental Health Act twice prior to the murder of Jodi. On one of those occasions, he was sectioned for an attack on his sister.

He had no alibi for his whereabouts on the 30th of June 2003 from approximately 1 p.m. to 1 a.m. It wasn't until he was widely accepted as being the "stocky man" seen following Jodi on Easthouses Road as she walked towards Roan's Dyke Path, that an alibi was created for him.

The days after the murder Joseph was absent. No mention of him from his granny, Alice, his mum, Judith, his sister, Janine, or his mum's partner, Alan Ovens despite the police being all over them. Joseph went into care, under the Mental Health Act, putting him out of reach of police questioning and scrutiny. It wasn't until five days later, and after Luke was the *"only suspect,* that the police spoke to him.

There were a lot of miraculous events in and around this time in and around Dalkeith. There were memory gains, sex changes, incredible medical break throughs, and even psychics. Alice Walker *"just knew"* to go to Roan's Dyke Path that fateful night. When asked in court why she went directly to Roan's Dyke Path she stated, *"I just did."*. When Jodi wasn't home for 10 p.m., which was not unusual as she was regularly much later that, Stephen Kelly and Judith, *"just had a feeling something was wrong"* and *"just knew something was up"*.

Cannabis resin, the drug that Nimmo Smith QC had attributed to the psychosis of Luke and led him to murder Jodi, and which made Joseph psychotic, paranoid and house bound, had all of a sudden brought about miraculous breakthroughs in mental health treatments and removed the paranoia from Joseph allowing him to leave the house.

Joseph had been smoking bucket bongs for days prior to the murder and on the day Jodi was murdered. So, it's a reasonable assumption, given his medical history, that he was or was going to be psychotic after such a session. He was certainly mentally unwell on the 1st of July, the day after the murder, although apparently not because of the bucket bongs and cannabis that he had been smoking prior to the murder, but because he was upset at what had happened to his sister.

The fantastic memories which were discovered and the realization of facts of events were incredible. Alan Ovens suddenly remembered it wasn't Janine who was in Judith's house when he returned from work but was Joseph.

Then Judith, who admitted having been on large vodkas all afternoon and evening on the day Jodi was murdered, could all of a sudden recall, after several previous statements and after the "stocky man" was brought to the attention of police, every small detail of what had happened that fateful day - and I do mean details. Every minute of the day and everything that happened, including what Joseph had been wearing as he slept upstairs in the home, despite previously claiming she knew he was home because she heard him moving about. The whole thing should have raised a red flag but police just accepted anything and everything without question.

When you couple this with the fact that Alice Walker told John Ferris and Gordon Dickie not to go forward to the police after they had made an appeal for the two men on the moped, it stinks of a cover up. Why in the world would a grandmother of a child who has been brutally murdered tell people who are witnessed at the locus at the time of the murder not to go forward to the police, unless she was protecting someone. In my opinion, Alice Walker should have been charged with perverting the course of justice.

Now Judith and Alice may have been merely protecting their son and grandson from being wrongly accused due to his mental health history. Judith was quoted as saying, *"thank goodness they don't know about Joseph's mental health problems"* and given what had happened to Luke because he was a bit weird, I can understand why people would want to protect their own in these circumstances. However, this was murder inquiry regarding their daughter and granddaughter, and they should have been honest and transparent.

Gordon Dickie and John Ferris, the "moped men", we know were at the locus at the police time of death as they parked their moped at the V in the wall and then `disappeared` from approximately 5 p.m. until 5.20 p.m. These two allege they didn't know where they had been or who they had seen in that time. Now we had memory loss in the case.

How can anyone seriously believe that these men, known to Jodi and who were advised not to come forward by Alice Walker, could not remember where they were five days earlier when their friend and relative was brutally murdered, at the very spot where they had parked their bike.

Gordon Dickie was a brutal thug, who had previous for bullying and beating women. During Luke's trial he was asked about his previous, however it was never really explored. It wasn't until 2012 that it became known that Dickie Jnr had also been charged with an assault, with severe injury and permanent disfigurement on a woman using an iron bar as a weapon.

We are to believe two men leave the locus, go to Dickie's home on Reed Drive, and minutes later the father, David Dickie, walked straight to the locus with nine working spaniels, lifting one over the wall as it was too old to jump through. He claims that his nine spaniels did not indicate towards Jodi, who was lying approximability seventeen metres away. Anyone who has any knowledge of working spaniels or dogs knows this is nonsense. The dogs would have been all over Jodi.

We know that Ferris and Dickie were the two men who arrived on the moped, but we do not know which two men left the locus and travelled to Reed Drive. We only have Ferris' and Dickie's word on this, and we know they are both liars.

Judith Jones was correct when she said that Ferris and Dickie Jnr were lying and covering up what happened that fateful day. Whether they murdered Jodi, or played a part, or know who did, only they know. But there is no doubt that they were involved in the murder in some way or another. One thing is for sure - if they had witnessed Luke Mitchell being involved in the murder of Jodi or being at the locus, they would have named him in a second.

Ferris and Dickie Jnr then go on to scrap the moped in the local scrap yard, *{everyone in the local area accepts this, but police did not investigate}* Ferris then cuts his own hair to change his appearance as, according to him, he didn't want to be mistaken for the stocky man or be wrongly accused. Then there were reports of burning clothes in and around Reed Drive, which was not an unusual event. Why these men were not charged with perverting the course of justice can only be explained by assuming it was because they helped police to discredit Luke with a character assassination.

In any other crime or police investigation these people would have been major suspects. There would have been search warrants, dawn raids, and serious questioning. In this case, the police respond by taking their associate, David Dickie, to the locus and ask him for his `expertise` on tracking. When they later found a blood-like substance on Dickie Snr's boot, they couldn't use the evidence as they had taken him to the locus. This was beyond negligent.

Both Dickies had been questioned about their sexual advances towards Jodi and police had mentioned that the killer could have been `sexually embarrassed`. Yet here was one of them helping police point the finger at Luke with a rant about footprints in adjacent field to the locus, and how they led to the tool hire place at Newbattle Road. Strangely, the police investigation hadn't turned up evidence of "Luke Mitchell's footprints" – the only claimed evidence was from Dickie.

The infamous interview with Ian Huntley springs to mind here. A guilty man joining the search party, then courting the media to inform them that they were important in helping solve the crime, all while pointing the police in the wrong direction. He would not be the first guilty man to join a search party and court the media while boasting to the neighbours how he had helped catch the killer. Babes in the Woods murderer, Russell Bishop and Ian Huntley are only a couple of examples who exhibited behaviour similar to Dickie Snr in this case.

I have never really believed James Falconer, the "`condom man", was guilty of murdering Jodi, However, his statement that he walked yards from his home to go into the woodland strip for a `clean wank` is utter nonsense, in my opinion.

The used condom containing his sperm and found fifteen meters away from where Jodi lay, should have been investigated and the person identified and eliminated, especially considering the police first thought Jodi had disturbed someone committing a sexual act. The fact that they did not trace Falconer for three years sums up the whole police operation.

Robert Greens, later known as the DaVinci Rapist, was visiting his sister on the 30th of June 2003 in cottages located a few hundred yards away from the locus. Greens was a heavy hash smoker, allegedly fifteen cannabis joints a day, age 25 in 2003, and from Mayfield. He was convicted in 2005 of brutally attacking and raping a young woman near the Rosslyn Chapel in Midlothian. A Dutch Student visiting the historical Rosslyn Chapel left to walk to the neighbouring town of Bonnyrigg. Greens drove past her, stopped the car, and threw her down an embarkment and savagely beat her. The victim's injuries were so horrific that the person who found her thought she had been hit by a car.

We have a psychotic and evil man, who would likely have known Dickie and Ferris as they were from the same area, a few hundred yards away from where hash selling men lived and where a wee girl is brutally murdered, yet there is no record of him ever being questioned or ruled out.

Jodi was beaten to a pulp, sustaining injuries consistent with being punched and kicked, dragged about and bludgeoned, but she fought back. Jodi fought for her life, so there is no doubt whatsoever that whoever attacked her would have had injuries or traces of the struggle. It a common misperception that Jodi was stabbed to death. That's untrue. Jodi was not only beaten, but strangled, and the strangulation rendered her unconscious.

Then someone, either the same person or another, stripped her, tied her hand/arms together and mutilated her body. The deep cut on the inside of her forearm was administered just before death *{perimortem}*. Livor mortis establishes that Jodi died while she was face down. She was then turned, and her throat, mouth, breast, and torso mutilated. The images will live with me forever.

To carry out such an attack and leave no trace of forensics or have no trace whatsoever on the attacker is impossible. There is not one person involved in this case over the past nineteen years who could tell me how such a crime could be committed without any forensic trace. These people included QC`s, lawyers, forensic scientists, pathologists, serious criminals and hunters with experience and knowledge in avoiding detection. Not one of them could give an explanation as to how this was possible, and that's because it`s not.

Moreover, Luke Mitchell was not, in my opinion, physically capable of carrying out the beating perpetrated upon Jodi. Generally speaking, the people who investigated this case and continue to do so, are middle class, have limited knowledge of the local area or culture, and don't have an understanding of the people.

There are some women from Dalkeith who are anything but a victim, as they would give as good as they got in a fight with any man. Jodi was from a rough background, and I don't say that with disrespect. I originate from Danderhall and a similar background. Jodi had a rough brother, sister, cousins, and all-round family so she was accustomed to fighting back to protect herself. On this occasion, the pathologist said she fought for her life and the attacker would have had marks from the fight.

If it was Luke who had attacked her, he would have had bruises or scratches from the fight. He had nothing, no marks or bruises on the face, body, or hands. We know Mark Kane had scratches on his face and we know that Joseph, Dickie Jnr, and Ferris weren't physically examined and weren't seen by the police until five days after the murder.

The person who battered and strangled Jodi was much more powerful and stronger than her. She was dragged and thrown about with punches and kicks to her face and head. Her brother Joseph, Dickie Jnr, Mark Kane, and Robert Greens all had the psychological make up, as well as the physical power, to have carried out such an attack. But the police focused on a fourteen-year-old boy.

The motive eventually, and I say eventually as the police first believed Jodi had disturbed a sexual deviant or someone sexually embarrassed, then maybe Jodi had refused sex to the killer, later became that Luke and Jodi, two fourteen-year-olds, had argued about him possibly having another girl friend and he had beaten, stripped, murdered, and mutilated her body. I find this suggestion ludicrous when I look at my thirteen-year-old grandson and his mates

A motive was never established because maybe there was no motive. It's possible someone just exploded and carried out this horrific crime for no other reason than mental illness or pure evilness, as some just do.

Nevertheless, Luke was taken to trial, found guilty by a Jury, and sentenced to a minimum term of twenty years. There was much that the Jury was not made aware of. Joseph Jones, or the stocky man, Mark Kane, and James Falconer to mention only three. They weren't made aware of the torturing of animals or the violent and psychotic behaviour of other suspects. They weren't aware of Kane's obsession with mutilated corpses or that he was on Newbattle Road where Fleming and Reed had seen a man that looked like Luke. However, it would not have mattered in my opinion, because of the role the media played. They pronounced him guilty before the trial even started.

What the jury believed is genuinely preposterous and astonishing. Only through emotions invoked by the heinous crime itself and the stirring of hate toward Luke from the media, could this have been possible.

How could he commit such a crime with no trace of forensics? Jodi had multiple wounds. The vast majority were physical wounds from a struggle, and yet when stripped and photographed, Luke showed no traces of having been in a struggle.

We then have to accept that a boy of fourteen, with no criminal experience in relation to DNA or forensics, walked down Roan's Dyke Path to the V in the wall, an eight-minute walk, persuaded Jodi over the wall, carried out a frenzied attack, strangled her, stripped her, tied her up, mutilated her, got to his home, another twenty-minute walk, and got rid of all forensics from his person, without leaving a trace in the home. All in under fifty minutes......Impossible!

The `missing knife` that the police had in their possession

and had photographed, was used to imply that this was the murder weapon, which is disrespectful to the murder of Jodi. She had been battered, bludgeoned, *{vast majority of Jodi injuries}* strangled until rendered unconscious, stripped, and tied up, and then mutilated. There is one wound on Jodi's arm which nearly cuts her hand off. The wound is very similar to a machete wound. It certainly could not have been inflicted by a legal pen knife.

The alleged burning of the parka coat in the wee fire in the back green is laughable if it wasn't so serious. The burner isn't capable of burning a coat of any description. If the pit was much larger and a coat was burned in it, there would have been forensic traces in the ashes and all over the garden. Anyone with any knowledge or experience in avoiding detection in crime by burning evidence would know this, including the investigating police officers. The police knew this but fed the nonsense to the public rather than investigating the murder of Jodi.

There are many criminals in prison who attempted to burn evidence using petrol, blowing up cars, etc., but left a tiny trace of DNA behind. However, we are expected to believe that a mother and son, both with no criminal experience, burnt a coat without a trace of petrol or accelerant and without leaving a hint of residue.

Saying the V in wall was the only way Jodi could have entered the woodland strip is just untrue. It is nothing more than an assumption that Jodi went through the V, and an assumption based on a lack of knowledge or investigation into the local area. There are several other ways, based on the last sighting Jodi on Easthouses Road, that she could have travelled that fateful day.

Moreover, the Roan's Dyke Path wall has several breaks in it which are much easier to go through to get into the woods. The only thing we know about the particular V in the wall, in relation to this case, is that a moped was parked there at the time the police claim Jodi was murdered, and two men escaped from there soon after.

Luke's dog, Mia, was an important part of his defence. Luke, Janine, Kelly, and Alice Walker claimed that the dog had reacted just past the V in the wall, by putting her paws up on the wall and sniffing the air. Sadly, for Luke, Walker, Janine, and Kelly all later changed their statements denying this ever happened. The jury didn't believe Luke and his description as to how his dog had reacted.

The fact that Mia was trained by a regimental Sergeant Major from the Royal Veterinary Corps didn't matter to his defence team. A man with more than thirty years of experience in selecting the pick of the litter and then training those pups for human and explosive detection, and who believed Mia was *"exceptional", was* never asked for an opinion.

German Shepherds boast about 225 million olfactory receptors, while Dachshunds have 125million. The more receptors the dog has, the better they are for finding humans and human remains, and well-trained Shepherds are 95% accurate.

While we are asked to dismiss the actions of an exceptional German Shepherd trained by an expert, we are also asked to believe that Dickie Snr went directly to the locus minutes after the alleged time of the murder, with his nine working spaniels, and they didn't react to Jodi's body lying approximately seventeen metres away and he didn't see anything....and the band played on ... believe it if you like.

These working dogs had spent their lives on the Lammer Muir Hills flushing out game in the bracken and to suggest they wouldn't smell or go to a body so close by is a lie. No person with knowledge of working dogs accept that this could have happened.

If telephone records had been obtained by the defence, or if the police hadn't been ever so selective in which records they chose to examine and pass over to the defence, they could have answered many questions which remain unanswered.

If the texts from Luke to Jodi at 4:38 p.m. had been retrieved they could have established exactly what plans they had made, instead of police making wild assumptions. If Luke was in his house when he texted Jodi to see if she was allowed out to play it couldn't have been him at Roan's Dyke Path as he wouldn't have had the time to get there. Seven minutes later he called the speaking clock, as he had done many times before according to records, and this was used as proof he was on his way to meet Jodi.

Then his calls to Judith's landline at 5:32 p.m. and 5:40 p.m. to find out where Jodi was, so soon after the estimated time of the murder of 5:15 p.m., was him setting up an alibi, according to the police. So now we are to believe a boy of fourteen, after brutally attacking and killing his girlfriend, had the level head to call her parent's house to set up an alibi seventeen minutes later as he was fleeing the scene. Absolute nonsense.

The whole thing was a farce and a setup, and the only phone records sought or disclosed, were the ones the police could fit into their narrative, irrespective of how ridiculous they were.

The whole thing was absurd, to the say least. But the media coverage had served its purpose. The "evil" Luke was pronounced guilty before he walked into Edinburgh High Court. The media convicted Luke Mitchell and hack reporters created a monster without a trace of evidence.

However, I believe what can break you can also make you. At long last, most of the media, the ones with nothing hide, are now highlighting the very strong possibility that Luke is a victim of a serious miscarriage of justice. The media helped create this miscarriage and now they can help bring about some kind of justice for both Jodi and Luke.

Having been involved in this case for eighteen years, with thousands of hours of consultations with criminal psychologists, criminologists, QC`s, lawyers, former police, investigative journalists, poachers, gamekeepers, and violent criminals, I can say without fear that I do not know who murdered Jodi Jones on the 30$^{\text{th of}}$ June 2003.

What I do know is that the police botched a murder investigation so badly that some professional people, understandably so, believe they did so deliberately to protect someone close to them.

Personally, I do not go that far, but there is no doubt that Lothian and Borders Police actions were scandalous. The destruction of the crime scene and the inept "investigation," and I use that word begrudgingly, were chaotic to say the least.

Based on a hunch and nothing more, the police made a child, a school boy, their one and only suspect from the start, and when their hunch was proven to be wrong when there were no forensic links, they relied on their `pals` in the media to step in with their smear campaign, spreading lies, and destroyed a wee boy and his family.

The person or persons who murdered Jodi are `beasts`. They can`t be right in the head, worse than any animal. But, in my opinion, the investigating team from Lothian and Borders Police and their friends in the media, who stitched up a child, aren't any better.

We have managed to secure the services of one of Scotland's top QC's who has promised their services pro bono if needed, to help secure access to the some of the forensic samples from this case in order that they can be re-examined or examined for the first time. There is strong opinion that there will be evidence which will prove who the killer or killers were. This isn't an easy task as the Crown have been refusing any access and it can take years to persuade the court to grant permission. But I'm sure that one day there will be some form of justice for Jodi Jones and Luke Mitchell.

No one knows who murdered Jodi, apart from the killer, killers, and the people who helped cover for them. Apart from them, all we know is that Jodi was last seen on Easthouses Road, being followed by her brother Joseph. We don't know where Jodi or Joseph went after that sighting. We do not know if Jodi went into the woods by the first entrance used by Falconer and Dickie Snr or walked into the woods another way.

We know Ferris and Dickie arrived at the locus {the V} around 5 p.m., but we don't know where they went, who they met, or what they did, while they left the bike parked against the wall. We know two men left on the moped at around 5:15 p.m. and travelled to Reed Drive. We do not know what happened behind that wall in the woodland strip on the 30th of June 2003, apart from Jodi being brutally attacked, murdered, and mutilated.

I'm of the opinion that when David Dickie went back to the V in the wall with his dogs, he went there after his son Gordon Dickie told him about what had happened, and being an experienced poacher and hunter with years of experience in avoiding detection from police and gamekeepers, David separated Jodi's body from where she was murdered to create a `false scent trial`. He did this to cover for his boy, and whether the son was directly involved in the murder or not, Dickie Jnr and John Ferris know who murdered Jodi and what happened that day. Dickie Snr then went back to where Jodi had been found and destroyed any chance of dogs from Yorkshire finding where Jodi was murdered by using a bleach like substance, which is common within hunting and poaching to protect a site.

An Offer

In 2013, Luke Mitchell and his mother took and passed a polygraph test, and I am willing to use proceeds from this book to pay for anyone willing to take a similar test to clear their name and stop people `pointing the finger at them`. I invite both Dickies, Ferris, Joseph, and anyone else to take a polygraph test.

"Here's freedom to them that wad read, Here's freedom to them that wad write! There's nane ever fear'd that the truth should be heard, but they whom the truth would indite". Robert Burns

Printed in Great Britain
by Amazon

17410825R00119